CHRIS WOODYARD

Illustrated by Landis Blair

ALSO BY CHRIS WOODYARD

Haunted Ohio: Ghostly Tales from the Buckeye State
Haunted Ohio II: More Ghostly Tales from the Buckeye State
Haunted Ohio III: Still More Ghostly Tales from the Buckeye State
Haunted Ohio IV: Restless Spirits
Haunted Ohio V: 200 Years of Ghosts
Spooky Ohio: 13 Traditional Tales
Ghost Hunter's Guide to Haunted Ohio
The Face in the Window: Haunting Ohio Tales
The Headless Horror: Strange and Ghostly Ohio Tales
The Ghost Wore Black: Ghastly Tales from the Past
The Victorian Book of the Dead
A Spot of Bother: Four Macabre Tales (Fiction)

Portions of this book may have appeared in *The Victorian Book of the Dead,* https://thevictorianbookofthedead.wordpress.com, http://hauntedohiobooks.com or https://mrsdaffodildigresses.wordpress.com.

First Printing

Printed in the United States of America
Design and Typesetting by Craig Ramsdell, RamsdellDesign.com
Illustrations by Landis Blair, landisblair.com

Library of Congress Control Number: 2023913459

Woodyard, Chris
A is For Arsenic: An ABC of Victorian Death Chris Woodyard
SUMMARY: A basic guide to Victorian mourning practices, defining and illustrating objects and themes of Victorian mourning with 19th- and early 20th-century primary sources.
ISBN: 978-0-9881925-4-6

1. Death –Social aspects—19th century
2. Mourning customs—19th century
3. Funeral rites and ceremonies—19th century

For Jessica, who was present at the creation.

ACKNOWLEDGEMENTS

My deepest thanks to the following for their help and encouragement:

Marsha Hamilton, friend and sorely-tried editor.

Suzie Lennox of mymacabreroadtrip.com

Simon Young of strangehistory.net and
my Boggart and Banshee podcast partner.

Landis Blair of landisblair.com

Craig Ramsdell of RamsdellDesign.com

Pat Latham of brprinters.com

Sarah Woodyard and Michael Ramsey

and John Woodyard
(who enjoyed the book in spite of himself.)

Introduction

I grew up shadowed by Victorian death. As a child, I haunted cemeteries, hopping over the fence of an overgrown graveyard behind my elementary school during recess to puzzle out inscriptions on lichen-covered stones from the 1820s.

When I was seven, I discovered a tiny 19th-century cemetery in a local woods. One of the stones was for "Sarah," who died aged seven. It was the first time I realized that children could die. I have been fascinated by Victorian mourning ever since.

After I wrote *The Victorian Book of the Dead,* I began to get questions about the fundamentals of Victorian mourning from followers of my social media, as they tried to untangle historical fact from urban legends on the internet.

A is for Arsenic is designed as an accessible, accurate, and at times, entertaining, introduction to the basics of Victorian mourning and death.

The book will also, hopefully, put to rest a few myths about Victorian mourning. With so much historical disinformation circulating, it seems a useful goal to make the customs of the past—often so different from our own—come alive.

A is for Arsenic unveils mourning traditions in the United States and Britain, with a few nods to France, in the years from about 1850 to 1920, with a concentration on the Golden Age of Crape—just after the American Civil War up to World War I. Here the term "Victorian" suggests cultural attitudes, rather than a strict chronology or geography. While there were calls for mourning reform from the eighteenth century onward, the elaborate rituals of Victorian mourning did not die with Queen Victoria in 1901. It took the mass casualties of the Great War to put them six feet under.

I became a resurrectionist about 33 years ago, digging up primary sources—Victorian and Edwardian newspapers, trade catalogues, magazines, literature, and humor—that give us a glimpse into 19th-century life and were invaluable in researching this book. When a mourning convention reaches the level of a newspaper joke, you may be fairly certain it was well known. However, the past is not always a pleasant place and some of the original sources found here make for very gruesome (or, to use a common 19th-century spelling, grewsome) reading.

Victorians have often been, unfairly in my view, accused of being morbidly obsessed with death. While we might diagnose Queen Victoria as suffering from what is now called "Complicated Grief," the people of the nineteenth century were exposed to the realities of death and dying far more than most of us will ever be. They had every right to be preoccupied with death and mourning conventions.

What can the so-called death-obsessed Victorians teach our death-averse culture? These were people like us, who cared, who mourned the frequent losses in their lives while trying to accept the inevitability of death, and who created mourning rituals—elaborate and sometimes burdensome—to provide meaning and comfort.

This book is an attempt to connect with the past, and, perhaps, to understand present grief. It shows that we are, in the end, not much different from the people of the past, in our lives and in our deaths—and in our universal longing for those who are not lost, but gone before.

Notes on Editing and Spelling.

There is a citation after each story. Citations from newspapers often list stories reprinted from other papers, which is why readers may see a newspaper citation for an incident that took place in a different state or country from the newspaper cited. Some stories have been edited for length. In that case, omitted text is noted with ellipses (...) Spelling, both British and American, has been retained from the original sources, except for obvious errors. Period newspapers often inserted headlines into the text for emphasis and these have been included. The rest of the language is as it came from the pen of the reporter. Please note that the sentiments expressed in these articles are not my own, but those of the original journalist or newspaper in which they appeared.

A is for Arsenic
Inheritance Powder
Serve it in chocolate
In coffee or chowder

If you were a Victorian murderer puzzling over which poison to choose, you could not go far wrong with arsenic. Cheap, colorless, tasteless, odorless, and readily available, arsenic was the ideal poison for the homicidally inclined. Arsenic's only drawback was that it needed to be dissolved in a hot liquid like chocolate or soup so that the victim would not notice its gritty texture. It was a versatile poison, equally useful for killing parasites in swine or for dispatching a parasitical partner.

The most common arsenic, called "white arsenic" or "arsenic trioxide," was sold as a powder, which was easily and fatally mistaken for flour or sugar. The poisonous powder, Paris Green, so-called because it had been used to kill rats in the sewers of Paris, was a key ingredient in insecticides and the popular commercial rat poison called "Rough on Rats." Arsenic was also found in medicines such as the tonic called "Fowler's Solution," and cosmetics like "Dr. Simm's Arsenic Complexion Wafers," conveniently raising doubts for coroners' juries as to whether a death was a deliberate or accidental poisoning. Liquid poisons were supposed to be kept in bottles with pointed surfaces or shaped like a coffin to reduce the chance of inadvertent ingestion.

A specific test for arsenic—the Marsh test—was invented by an English chemist named James Marsh in 1836, but its availability did not deter determined poisoners.

For obvious reasons arsenic was referred to as "inheritance powder," or, if one wished to be elegantly euphemistic, *"poudre de succession."* The term is frequently mentioned in articles about a plague of poisonings in the late 1800s, which compare those murders to the crimes of the notorious 17th-century French poisoners the Marquise de Brinvilliers and La Voisin.

In 1851, the Arsenic Act of Great Britain required soot or indigo to be added to arsenic so it would not be mistaken for flour or sugar. Purchasers also had to sign the poisons register at the pharmacy, giving their name and why they wanted the arsenic. To kill vermin was the usual excuse; unwanted spouses and rich relatives seemed to fall under that heading.

The dangers of arsenic were not confined to deliberate poisonings. The arsenical green dye, known as Scheele's Green, was reported to have poisoned wearers of green garments, as well as those occupying rooms with green wallpapers, the makers of artificial leaves and flowers, and readers of green-bound books. Other verdant agents of death were candles, carpets, artificially colored peas, candies, and pickles.

> A young Viennese woman bought a brilliantly [*sic*] green silk bodice. The color came out with perspiration, pimples appeared, and she died with symptoms of mineral poisoning.
>
> —*The Cincinnati [OH] Enquirer,* 17 October, 1908: p. 11.

> **Poisoned by Green Dye**
>
> Anderson, Ind. September 1. Raymond Wood, the contortionist, who is well known in the profession and whose home is in this city, is lying at 83 South Jackson street in a precarious condition caused by wearing green tights which had been colored with green dyes.
>
> —*Evening News* [San Jose, CA], 1 September, 1894: p. 1.

Those who manufactured fashionable trifles colored with arsenic suffered terribly.

> **THE POISONED GRASS.**
>
> **Horrors of Fashion—The Murder of the Innocents.**
>
> English ladies have taken to wearing in their hats little tufts of artificial grass sprinkled with glass beads, to imitate dewdrops. In the manufacture of this kind of adornment a virulent poison, called Scheele's green is employed, which is a compound of arsenic and copper. The color is applied by women and children, who earn only a miserable pittance by the work, and who, by inhaling the fumes of the poison become dangerously sick and even die. A reporter of the London *Daily Telegraph* has been inquiring into the matter, and an article in that paper says:
>
> "Our commissioner visited a family engaged in the preparation of this grass of death. Little, pinched, white faces, dull eyes circled with red, inflamed lids; a perpetual catarrh, and a constant

wheeze in the throat, marked every member in the group...Those painful symptoms excite little notice; they always occur when a large order for grass is obtained by such a household. What is more serious in the experience of these scatterers of deadly dewdrops on deathful herbage is *when the ears bleed*. 'It ain't a good sign; many in our line gets it,' said the mother of the family... and the little girl beside her who had the bleeding ears stopped them by a piece of wadding out of her brother Joe's cap, and went on too. Sneezing and coughing, and mopping their running eyes in the midst of the arsenic dust, the family could make twelve shillings a week out of the business. They had to work late and early though, and work 'all hands' bleeding, or not bleeding, coughing or not coughing, to earn as much as this."

—*The Peoples' Tribune* [Jefferson City, MO], 25 October, 1871: p. 4.

Sometimes the method of arsenic poisoning was more subtle.

Poisonous Candles.

Recently a lady, living in a fashionable quarter of Paris, became ill in such a way that she was supposed to be suffering from slow poisoning. The physician who was called in, one morning found the water placed by her bed covered with a thin film of arsenic. She had been in the habit of reading in bed, and the candles she used having been examined, were found to be of dazzling whiteness... caused by the admixture of arsenic, which, being volatilized during the process of combustion, had poisoned the air of the room. These candles...looked well, and gave a clear, bright flame. But people who used them became affected with strange symptoms... [I]t was found that the candles derived their attractive qualities from arsenic being used in their manufacture in such quantities as to be dangerous to health, if not to life. The fact was made public, the new candles being nicknamed "corpse candles".... [See DEATH TOKEN.]

—*The Manufacturer and Builder*, March, 1877: p. 54.

In what seems to us an almost criminally casual way, books on domestic economy recommended leaving arsenic mixed with flour in cupboards to tempt rats. Further, those books failed to suggest labeling the saucer of poisoned flour to alert the household of the danger, with the result that this lethal mixture often found its way into pancakes, pies, and puddings.

FIVE ARE POISONED

Gravy Blamed for Illness of Wooster (O.) Family.

Wooster, O., May 6. Five members of the family of Frank Snell, living near Canaan, are recovering from poisoning.

Snell mixed poison with flour to kill rats. One of the women used the flour by mistake for making gravy.

—*Cincinnati [OH] Post,* 6 May, 1921: p. 1.

The family of John Retalick, of Waterloo, narrowly escaped death last week from eating biscuits containing arsenic. A saucer of flour mixed with the deadly drug, had been prepared for rats and placed behind the flour-barrel. In sweeping, one of the girls placed the saucer on the head of the flour barrel and left it there. Next morning when Mrs. Retalick went to make bread for breakfast she turned the contents of the saucer in with the other flour supposing it to be the one she had dipped flour with. It came near being a fatal mistake. The family all partook of the bread and soon became deathly sick. Medical aid was speedily procured from Beetown and under the prompt and skillful treatment of the doctor all were soon relieved from the overdose of arsenic.

—*Lancaster [WI] Teller,* 20 September, 1888: p. 1.

The Last Word

Victorian flypapers were made with arsenic. Testimony at the sensational murder trial of Florence Maybrick in 1889, described how she soaked flypapers in water to extract the poison she was said to have administered to her husband.

B is for Bier
Owned by the Parish
A modest death trolley
Nothing too garish

A bier was a hand-carried stretcher or hand-cart on which a body or coffin was moved to the grave.

> Up to the eighteenth century, coffined burials were the exception, the corpse being interred simply in its shroud. It was customary, therefore, for each parish to possess a bier and a shell or coffin to rest upon it, for carrying the body to the grave.
>
> —*The Essex Review: An Illustrated Quarterly Record of Everything of Permanent Interest in the County.* Miss C. Fell Smith, editor. Vol. XXXV, 1926: p. 160.

Most biers were sober, utilitarian articles, designed to carry the dead to church and the grave with as little trouble as possible. They had a rural aesthetic, as homely as a wheelbarrow or hay wain, reflecting their function of trundling the dead to the field where they would await the last harvest.

Biers were the property of the parish and traditionally were stored in the church building or on church ground, so they were a familiar, if slightly sinister sight.

> Beside the gate stood a bier,—a lean, black frame with four handles. It stood there winter and summer, always waiting, always ready. Some seasons the grass grew up rank and tall around it, as if to hide the thing from passers-by, but it never could be lost. Death was sure to find it.
>
> —*Summer-savory: Gleaned from Rural Nooks in Pleasant Weather.* Benjamin Franklin Taylor. 1879: p. 80.

In a Pembrokeshire parish, the church bier functioned as an omen of death.

> While on the subject of warnings and death omens, I may mention a curious tradition connected with an old church I know in Pembrokeshire. In a corner of the building is kept the bier used at funerals; and it is reported that always just before any death

> occurs in the parish, this bier is heard to creak loudly, as though a heavy burden had been laid upon it.
>
> *Stranger Than Fiction, Being Tales from the Byways of Ghosts and Folk-Lore*. Mary L. Lewes. 1911: p. 218.

Wheeled biers were often used to transport corpses in Victorian parishes. These varied in style from very simple, baggage-wagon affairs to glassed and plumed miniature hand-powered hearses, embellished with gothic tracery or spires. They seem to have been more popular in Britain than in the United States.

There was controversy about whether it was more proper to have pall-bearers carry a coffin to the grave or to have it carried or wheeled on a bier. Some people clung to the old ways of corpse-carrying:

> In resistance to all changes in religious matters, the dalesmen are very stubborn. At one time many of the lesser churches had no burial-grounds about them: the dead had to be taken many miles to bury. Wheeled vehicles were practically unknown, and the coffins had to be carried either on horseback or by the neighbours....When a wheeled bier was suggested in order that the way to the churchyard might be somewhat easier for the friends of the departed, one old man strenuously objected. He would not give a penny piece: "If t' neighbours are not willing to carry me to t' church, why, then I'll walk!"
>
> —*Odd Yarns of English Lakeland: Narratives of Romance, Mystery and Superstition Told by the Dalesfolk.* William Thomas Palmer. 1914: p. 90.

> There stands in a dark corner, by the vestry door, a long wooden object, slatted and lifted on four feet from the ground, with poles projecting from the corners. This is a bier. It was to have been the parish bier, having been built to that end by the last incumbent of the church. Those, however, for whose use it was intended would have none of it. A bier was not to their taste. Since the memory of man they had gone to their last home on the arms of bearers; and so, by the help of Heaven and their own determination they still do and still will continue to do. Hence it is that the bier stands unused in an

unused corner of the church, a lasting witness to the sagacity of the islanders in deciding for themselves when to let well enough alone.

—"A Holy Island Pilgrimage." Eugenia Skelding.
The Atlantic Monthly, March, 1896: pp. 332-333.

In the Hertfordshire village of Bushey, a trade association of undertakers decided to ban wheeled biers, which were siphoning off their hearse business.

> One of the most unusual of the petty tyrannies that result from trade combinations has come to light in an English village, Bushey. It appears that the working people and others of Bushey have a wisely established system of "walking funerals," which not only save expense but add to the simplicity and solemnity of burial ceremonies. In these "walking funerals" a wheeled bier is used. It was presented to the town of Bushey some eighteen years ago by a lady who wished to save the members of the community the expense of "costly horses, hearse and carriages." Recently, however, the Rector of Bushey received a letter from the secretary of the local centre of the Undertakers' Association, who said; "It is undesirable for wheel-biers to be used for funerals and removals, and I am directed to notify you that our members will refuse to use a bier outside any church, churchyard or cemetery after June 30." In reply the Rector wrote:
>
> > This means the depriving the public of the use of the public biers, and the forcing them to use the very expensive hearse with their thoroughbred black horses. No undertaker dare, I suppose, to refuse to obey this arbitrary order of the association. To do so would be to find himself boycotted, and unable to obtain the necessary furniture and requirements for conducting funerals. The Rector added that even the Guardians of the Poor are subjected to the association's decree and cannot use their own bier.
>
> The Undertakers' Association made response that it did not desire in any way to interfere with walking or economical funerals,

> but that it objected to the instability of the wheeled bier. In view of the long period over which the bier has been in use, the association, which doubtless has considered the effects of competition, in this letter put forward a very thin explanation.
>
> —*Southland Times* [Invercargill, NZ], 22 September, 1920: p. 4.

Naturally, the name of the death stretcher lent itself to jokes.

> "That was a severe coughing fit," said a sexton to an undertaker, as they were drinking together.
>
> "Oh, it is nothing save a little ale which went down the wrong way," replied the undertaker.
>
> "Ah, that's just like you," said the sexton. "you always lay the coffin on the bier."
>
> —*New Zealand Truth* [Wellington, NZ], 26 September, 1914: p. 2.

The Last Word

The stand on which a corpse or coffin is placed at a morgue or during a wake or a funeral is also called a bier.

> [I]t is to be borne in mind that in Frankfort and Munich it has been the custom for many years to expose the dead as long as possible on biers surrounded with flowers, in a public place, with bell-wires or strings attached to their fingers, so that the slightest movement would summon an attendant.
>
> —*A Treatise on Hygiene and Public Health*, Volume II. Albert Henry Buck. 1879: p. 452.

C is for crape

The fabric of woe

Wear it for one year

From head down to toe

"Crape on the door" was generally the first sign that death had come to a household. A scarf of crape—black for an adult, white for a child or the unmarried—was tied to the knob or door knocker to indicate that there had been a bereavement.

> [S]ome one is dead, and it is the custom to put crape on the door—a custom beautiful in itself, infinitely beautiful if we look upon the insignia as one of hope and glad acquiescence in a summons to rest.
>
> "Someone is resting from sorrow and pain.
> Happy where earth's conflicts enter not in.
> One more departed to heaven's bright shore
> Ring the bell softly, there's crape on the door."...
>
> We start and walk with slow step and bated breath, as the very wave of crape meets our eyes, and we shudder instinctively in the bright sunshine....Custom has decreed that we shall thus inform the passer-by that death is present, and the solemn badge of the shadowy ambassador guards the portal from all idle intrusion. No social visits are paid to the house that shows that ensign; nor do people linger idle in the vicinity of the house that is thus set apart from its neighbors.
>
> The sombre pall of black crape on the door assures us that one of mature years has "passed over," but for a young person or a little child, white—the emblem of purity—is used, but it tells the same sad story....
>
> —*The Times-Picayune* [New Orleans, LA], 12 March, 1882: p. 3.

The hanging of crape on the door was a well-known, yet terrifying, symbol for a death in the household. We can have no conception of the shock, fear, and even horror that crape on the door evoked from those who saw it.

> "It was so closely associated with death in my young days that a touch of it sent chills down my spine."
>
> —*Vancouver [British Columbia, Canada] Daily World*, 30 October, 1920: p. 4.

> He had come within half a block of his home, on the opposite side of the street from it, when he saw something white on its door-bell knob. He imagined he saw the object sway gently in the breeze. Gazing intently on it, he had walked a dozen paces when of a sudden he felt a sinking in his heart, an indefinable impression of fear, of poignant grief and desolation. In another instant the feeling had transplanted into words, "My God, it's crape, Arthur is dead," and the breath seemed to leave his body.
>
> —*Cincinnati [OH] Commercial Tribune,* 4 November, 1890: p. 2.

Crape was truly the fabric of woe. As an instant marker of bereavement, crape had "brand recognition." It had no other purpose than to convey the sad news that a house or wearer was in mourning.

The reader will notice that the spelling "crape" is used in this book. This was the most common 19th-century spelling, both in England and the United States. There is a modern idea that "crape" with an "a" was only used by the Victorians when they meant mourning fabric; and "crepe" with an "e" was used only for fashionable fabrics. An extensive survey of word usage does not support that belief. On both sides of the Atlantic, mourning crape might be spelled with an "a" *or* an "e." Sometimes both spellings appear in a single article. It is the context, not the spelling, which indicates that a fabric is for mourning.

Crape was a fabric, made of silk, wool, or a blend of the two, that was run between heated rollers to give it a distinctive crimped, mottled pattern. Its dull finish made it suitable for mourning attire; nothing shiny was to be worn in deep mourning. The fabric had long been used for royal and aristocratic mourning, which gave it a fashionable cachet. The notion that crape was a requirement for showing proper respect to the dead was emphasized in scores of etiquette books and fashion columns, which reinforced consumer fears about not mourning "correctly."

> **For Young Widows.**
>
> A young widow, who... fears that she may be the cynosure of critical eyes, sends the following appeal to *Vogue*:

> "Please give advice for mourning for a young widow. What is the correct hat and veil? Are elbow sleeves good taste? What collar and cuffs are worn? What materials and trimmings? Give model for a traveling coat."
>
> It is pleasant to know that in the darkness of her affliction Young Widow is not to be left without a gleam of informing light. She pines to be correct. *Vogue* gives her information of so careful a character that, if she is not a model of proper mourning, the onus must be upon her own soul.
>
> —*Nashville [TN] Banner,* 4 August, 1906: p. 22.

Much of the anxiety over "correct" mourning was the fact that mourning for women was performative, demonstrating both family status and suitable commemoration of the dead. Women were the subject of harsh scrutiny over both mourning dress and behavior.

> It is well to have some established customs as to visiting and dress in order that the gay and the heartless may in observing them avoid that which shocks every one—an appearance of lack of respect to the memory of the dead—that all society may move on in decency and order, which is the object and end of the study of etiquette.
>
> —*Manners and Social Usages.*
> Mary Elizabeth Wilson Sherwood. 1918: p. 248.

> [A] wife's mourning for her husband is the most conventionally deep mourning allowed, and every one who has seen an English widow will allow that she has made a hearse of herself....In this country [the United States] a widow's first mourning dresses are covered almost entirely with crape, a most costly and disagreeable material, easily ruined by the dampness and the dust—a sort of penance and mortification dress, very ugly and very expensive....
>
> —*Harper's Bazaar,* 13 August, 1881: p. 514.

For most of the nineteenth century, Samuel Courtauld & Company, of Essex, England, held a virtual monopoly on the fabric's production. Crape was not produced in the United States, but had to be imported.

It was expensive, faded easily, spotted badly in the rain, and had an unpleasant smell. Physicians railed against its use, declaring that its dyes and fixatives were toxic and its color depressing. Yet, largely due to Courtauld's aggressive marketing of Courtauld crape as a brand, it was universally embraced as the only choice for mourning.

> Courtauld has won his preeminence in crape-making...There may be other crapes as good as Courtauld's. Nobody knows that there are; and few are willing to take the risk of them. Indeed careful merchants buy crapes as you do, not on their own judgment, but on faith in the makers.
>
> Philadelphia uses crape more profusely than any other city but London; and Philadelphia ladies are very exacting as to certain qualities in it....
>
> These local peculiarities of taste add much to the task of the merchant, who undertakes to gratify them. We have the advantage of a great trade; and are justified in keeping every grade, shade, and form of crape that is wanted here. We keep none but Courtauld's....
>
> JOHN WANAMAKER.
>
> —*The Times* [Philadelphia, PA], 31 January, 1882: p. 4.

Black was so often a fashionable color that crape was the only reliable way to tell if a gown was being worn for mourning.

> In fact, so very fashionable and elegant is modern mourning that the lavish use of crape in its initial stages is an absolute necessity in order to distinguish it from an ordinary black costume, such as may be seen by the score in an hour's turn on any fashionable thoroughfare.
>
> —*The Ottawa [Ontario, Canada] Journal*, 18 February, 1895: p. 4.

> As to the wearing of crape, it is a matter of individual taste; but considering how universally black is worn for ordinary occasions, it is all the more necessary, when it is worn for actual mourning, that it be more or less trimmed with crape.
>
> —*New-York [NY] Tribune*, 27 July, 1899: p. 5.

Etiquette books and columns gave conflicting advice about how long to wear crape. [See APPENDIX.] Times differed in England and France and it was frequently noted that the United States did not have a well-defined tradition, so the bereaved mourned longer than required elsewhere.

> To many who sorrow deeply, and who regard the crape and solemn dress as a mark of respect to the dead, it is deemed almost a sin for a woman to go into the street, to drive, or to walk, for two years, without a deep crape veil over her face. It is a common remark of the censorious that a person who lightens her mourning before that time "did not care much for the deceased"; and many people speak of the fact that a widow or an orphan wore her crape two years as much to her credit.
>
> —*Harper's Bazaar,* 13 August, 1881: p. 514.

Somewhat surprisingly, fashions in mourning changed as often as ordinary styles, which lent new meaning to the expression "one might as well be dead as to be out of the fashion." Widows were particularly criticized for even the mildest of flirtatious behavior, yet the fashion pages both ridiculed and promoted the notion of coquettish mourning fashions with headlines and articles such as the following:

PRETTY WIDOWS
How to Mourn a Loss Becomingly and Properly.
Materials and Styles Which Are Quite the Thing.
These Suggestions May Make the Mourner Pretty and Sincere.

—*Oakland [CA] Tribune,* 30 January, 1892: p. 9.

> Why somber crape should make a bright woman more mirthfully soubrettish we cannot tell; but unless her heart be securely anchored in the grave of her husband, the conjunction of crape and a widow's cap will make the average woman a coquette in spite of herself.
>
> —*Detroit [MI] Free Press,* 29 August, 1883: p. 3.

> The best mourning—speaking from the standpoint of good taste—is extremely simple in style but fashioned of the finest materials. Yards and yard of trailing crepe, heavily bordered handkerchiefs and rattling strings of black beads are left to the nouveau riches and the woman of breeding and distinction affects simple costumes perfectly made yet guiltless of frivolous outlines or a conspicuous and ostentatious use of crepe.
>
> This is not saying that mourning must, to be in good taste, be also dull, dreary and elderly. There are many ways of adding charm and even coquetry to the mourning costume—as the French who are adepts at this art, have discovered. Their mourning is an exquisitely skillful combination of dignity and subdued coquetry; yet no other mourning is so loaded with crepe as that of the French widow—and especially the youthful French widow. As a matter of fact there are few women to whom mourning is not becoming. The rich, simple black garb lends a refining spirituelle suggestion to the face and makes the figure more slender and graceful in effect, and it is the exceptional woman of whom it is not said, during her period of bereavement, "how becoming mourning is to her!"... [N]o trimming gives the dull black mourning costume such richness and elegance as crepe; and in France the coquetry of the youthful mourning costume increases in direct ratio with the amount of crepe employed in its garnishment.
>
> —*The Journal* [Meriden, CT], 30 April, 1913: p. 14.

The bereaved were always advised to buy the best quality of mourning. "Shabby mourning" was unthinkable for the fashionable.

> It's rather odd, but it's true, that the more some materials cost the cheaper they are, and this especially applies to crape. A good crape may be worn for a long time, dressed and redressed, and redressed again, and it always looks as good as new, while a cheap quality of crape has the unpleasant fashion of growing rusty in a very short

> time and looking like mitigated woe and suggesting nothing so much as grief that will not survive a rainy day.
>
> —*The Burlington [VT] Free Press,* 24 October, 1891: p. 7.

In addition to its role in fashionable mourning, crape was also used to drape public buildings in mourning for public figures and was sometimes used in political or economic protests.

For all the fear that crape on the door inspired, it also moved joke writers to a bit of gallows humor.

> "Did you carry that prescription to old Mrs. Smith last night?" said a doctor to his office-boy.
>
> "Yessir."
>
> "Did she take it?"
>
> "Yessir."
>
> "How do you know?"
>
> "Crape on the door this morning."
>
> —*Evening Star* [Dunedin, NZ], 27 January, 1887: p. 4.

The Last Word

Although in some communities it was a sign of respect to buy new mourning for each death in a family, it has been suggested by many dress historians that Victorians believed that it was unlucky to keep crape in the house after the period of mourning was ended. There seems to be no contemporary folklore to this effect and the notion seems contradicted by the many receipts for refurbishing crape and references, even in jokes, to putting crape away for another mournful occasion.

> **TO RESTORE CRAPE.**
>
> If you have a black crape veil which has lost its crinkle hang it out doors some day when there is a drizzling rain. After it has been well dampened fold it and put it under a mattress over night. It will be wonderfully improved in the morning.
>
> —*The Colfax Chronicle* [Grant Parish, LA], 27 October, 1894: p. 3.

Freshening Crape

If you are called upon to freshen crape, you can make it look like new by proper steaming. All sewing and threads should be taken out, and the crape thoroughly brushed. It is then steamed for some time over a steamer. The best qualities may be rolled about a round stick and fastened. Lay this roll over a boiler of steaming water and let it remain several hours, say four or five. After this put it to dry for twenty-four hours, or even longer, and you will be more than pleased with the result.

—*The Illustrated Milliner*, November, 1906: p. 27.

Bridget: Ma'am, I've took the crape off'n the door. What will I do with it?

Widow: Put it away carefully, Bridget. It has already served on two of these melancholy occasions, and we cannot tell what may happen.

—*The Daily Nonpareil* [Council Bluffs, IA], 1 January, 1887: p. 6.

D for Death Token
Dire omen of yore
Dogs howling; clocks stopping
A knock at the door....

The nineteenth century seemed obsessed by death tokens, those ominous signs that someone was about to die. It may be that the religious sentiment of the era, which emphasized being prepared to meet thy God, made knowing the day or the hour of one's demise desirable. Perhaps it was strangely reassuring to know that advance warning of that important event would allow the doomed to set their earthly affairs in order. Many death token stories speak of preparations: a coffin bought, a will made, a shroud or burial clothes chosen, and farewells said. Or maybe it was just human nature to like a good yarn about a premonition. It was said that even President Abraham Lincoln reported having dreams that seemed to predict his death.

Death tokens took many forms: the shrieking or knocking of the banshee, birds flying into the house or tapping at the window, a picture falling off the wall, a ticking in the wall known as "the death watch," or funereal visions of a coffin or crape on the door.

Phantom funerals were a particularly elaborate form of death token. The viewer would either see or feel a funeral procession passing by that predicted a real funeral soon to occur.

> Some years ago I had the strange yet true experience of meeting a phantom funeral. One Sunday morning, returning from church I saw a funeral cortege coming towards me, its glass hearse bearing the coffin on which lay many very beautiful wreaths. It was followed by two mourning coaches. As it approached, I paused to watch it pass by. As the hearse drew nearer to where I was standing, it, for a moment, remained still ere it passed on. Attracted by the many beautiful flowers, I turned to some ladies who had been walking close behind me from the church, and inquired if they knew whose funeral it might be. They looked at me in blank surprise and told me there had been no funeral whatever passing. I looked down the long country road—the cortege had vanished.

The next day, I received a message from a London church, where he whom I should have married was a clergyman...that he had died from a sudden heart attack on the Sunday morning.

—*Warnings from Beyond Told by "Daily News" Readers.*
S. Louis Giraud. 1927: p. 42.

Corpse candles were phantom lights seen coming to or from a house about to be visited by death.

The Corpse Candle is always and invariably a death-warning. It sometimes appears as a stately flambeau, stalking along unsupported, burning with a ghastly blue flame. Sometimes it is a plain tallow 'dip' in the hand of a ghost, and when the ghost is seen distinctly it is recognised as the ghost of some person yet living, who will now soon die... According to the belief of some sections, the size of the candle indicates the age of the person who is about to die, being large when it is a full-grown person whose death is foretold, small when it is a child, still smaller when an infant. Where two candles together are seen, one of which is large and the other small, it is a mother and child who are to die. When the flame is white, the doomed person is a woman; when red, a man.

—*British Goblins.* Wirt Sikes. 1881: p. 239.

Striking a Corpse Candle.

A clergyman...had a son who came home one night very late and found the doors locked against him. Not wishing to disturb his father and mother...he went to the man-servant's bedroom, which was over the stable. He could not awake the man-servant, but while standing over him he saw a small light issue from his nostrils. He followed it...on to the road which led up to the parish church. After following the corpse candle for some time, the young man, just to see what would happen, struck at it with his stick. It burst into sparks, but afterwards reunited...it finally disappeared in the churchyard.

Not long afterwards the man-servant died; at his funeral the bier broke at the spot where his master's son had struck at the corpse candle, and the coffin fell to the ground.

—*The Welsh Fairy Book*. W. Jenkyn Thomas. 1907: p. 287.

The shroud was also regarded as an infallible, if nuanced, death token in stories of second sight. It was a literal sliding scale of death: the higher on the figure that the shroud appeared, the sooner death would occur.

[At harvest time, a Mr McKinnon pointed out an especially efficient young woman reaper to the foreman.]

This man, who was said to have the gift of the 'second sight,' stedfastly [*sic*] regarded her for a moment or two, and then remarked—

'She is, indeed, a clever worker. Poor girl! I am sorry to say that this will be her last harvest.'

'What do you mean?' I asked.

'Why, that she will be dead in less than three months; her winding-sheet is already high upon her breast....

"Strange to say, about the time specified by [him], the poor girl took fever and died."

—*Ghostly Visitors: A Series of Authentic Narratives.* "Spectre Stricken." [William Stainton Moses.] 1882: p. 113.

The sight or sound of a phantom hearse was also a deadly omen.

This lady, who, by the way, persists that she is not at all superstitious, declares that some days before her mother's death she distinctly saw a hearse roll up to the door. The hearse was drawn by white horses. This vision made a deep impression upon her; so much so that upon relating it the next morning she remarked that she knew some one in the family would die very soon. Again she had seen this strange vision shortly before the death of her husband some years previous.

—*Boston [MA] Herald,* 7 April, 1889: p. 18.

As was the howling of a dog at night.

Black Dog Heralds Death.

Fond Du Lac, Wis., March 5. Superstitious folk in Fond du Lac are greatly concerned at the actions of a black dog, which for weeks past has occasionally appeared in the streets at dead of night howling dismally. It is alleged that the appearance of the canine has always been followed by a death in the neighborhood that it chooses for its nocturnal lamentations.

—*Hobart [OK] Daily Republican,* 5 March, 1908: p. 4.

The first [death token] I noticed was a large black dog piteously howling in front of a neighbor's door. I made a note of it: it was Wednesday and on Friday the master of the house was hurt at his work: he had both thighs broken, and was badly crushed as well. He died on the Sunday following....

One night, I was returning home from my office, when I saw a large sable collie dog howling at the door of a doctor's surgery. I thought to myself that it would be a sign of one of his patients that would be passing on, so I thought no more about it, but in about a week after, the doctor's nephew, who had been operated upon, died: he was a boy about six years old: he had come from a foreign country to be operated upon by his uncle. I could quote over two hundred cases, but the above will suffice.

—*How to Converse with Spirit Friends.*
Alexander Verner, F.A.I.P. 1904: pp. 32-35.

Birds straying into the house were thought to be deadly omens. Conversely, birds who abandoned their traditional nesting places, particularly rooks or other corvids, inevitably foretold death.

BIRDS AND HUMAN DEATH.

There appears to be good ground for believing that birds possess a sense of approaching death in a human being.

A friend of mine lived in a house standing in extensive grounds. At the back of the house were a number of trees in which the rooks built their nests regularly during the first six years. On the seventh year no nests were built. In the winter my friend's daughter died. In the eighth year, and during the five succeeding years, the rooks returned and built regularly. On the thirteenth year they again deserted, and during that year my friend's wife died. The rooks returned the following year and continued to build for three years, when they again deserted. That year my friend died. The following spring the rooks again returned to the rookery. A.C. (Bude).

—*T.P.'s and Cassell's Weekly*. 11 September, 1926: p. 638.

It was a common convention to stop household clocks at the time of death. "Sad Hour" funeral flower arrangements and coffin plates also noted the exact moment of dissolution. [See GLOSSARY.] It is possible that these practices influenced the many stories about clocks as death tokens: striking out of turn, suddenly chiming after not running for years, and stopped clocks, immortalized in the song "Grandfather's Clock,"

But it stopp'd short—never to go again—
When the old man died.

They have a genuine grandfather's clock in Maryland, at the residence of the late Thos. M. Calvert, in Cecil county. The clock had been running for twenty-one years without repairs. When Mr. Calvert died, the folks looked at the clock to note the moment of his death. The clock had stopped, and they can't make it run again.

—*The Atchison [KS] Daily Champion*, 31 January, 1880: p. 2.

THIS OLD CLOCK FORETOLD DEATH

Uncanny Actions of an Ancient Timepiece at Reading.

Reading, November 26. A few days ago Elmer B. Mosser, the 14-year-old son of Mr. and Mrs. Benneville G. Mosser, of Mohnsville, Berks county, died of diphtheria. He was buried and his parents are now convinced that his death was foretold by an old clock, which was on a mantel in Elmer's room.

Mrs. Mosser said: "Shortly after Mr. Mosser and I were married we were presented with a common kitchen clock. For the past year or more the clock has been out of repair and has stood on the mantel in Elmer's room. About 6 weeks ago, as we were retiring, we were startled to hear the old clock strike "one." Elmer directed attention to the striking of the clock and marveled at it. Two weeks later it again struck "one;" then several days later it once more struck "one." Never more than one, and when it struck the third time my husband and I certainly considered it a bad omen. Our worst fears were realized, because Elmer was taken sick with diphtheria and he died at 1 o'clock in the morning.

It has struck three times since his funeral. In the meantime our 10-year-old daughter, Mabel, developed symptoms of diphtheria. I had turned the hands of the clock in order to prevent it striking, but it did no good. If it strikes again I will demolish it."

—*The Times* [Philadelphia, PA], 27 November, 1900: p. 4.

One of the most fascinating tokens of death was the phantom sound of a coffin being made: sawing, planing, and nailing.

The Tolaeth is an ominous sound, imitating some earthly sound of one sort or another, and always heard before either a funeral or some dreadful catastrophe. Carpenters of a superstitious turn of mind will tell you that they invariably hear the Tolaeth when they are going to receive an order to make a coffin; in this case the sound is that of the sawing of wood, the hammering of nails, and the turning of screws, such as are heard in the usual process of making a coffin. This is called the 'Tolaeth before the Coffin.'

—*British Goblins.* Wirt Sikes. 1880: p. 225.

The Last Word

The banshee, a female spirit which shrieked, keened or knocked to announce that a death was coming, was sometimes said to only visit members of certain noble Irish or Scottish clans. Other lore says that each family has its own personal banshee.

E for Embalming
Pumped through the veins
Arsenical fluid
Preserves the remains

In 1775, a quack dentist, Martin Van Butchell, decided on a novel sales gimmick: he had the corpse of his wife embalmed and displayed in his London shop to attract customers. This was the first known use of the injection of chemical preservatives into the arteries to preserve a corpse.

In the United States, arterial embalming did not become common until the Civil War. A Union Army physician, Dr. Thomas Holmes, developed the technique of replacing a corpse's blood with arsenic-filled fluid. Many families wanted their loved ones' remains brought home for burial. Embalming, which was then quite costly, helped to achieve this.

The American journalist, George Alfred Townsend, who worked as a war correspondent during the American Civil War, reported on his conversation with a battlefield embalmer. The man was candid about profiteering off the high-ranking dead:

> In the misty dawn I saw the maimed still lying on the ground, wrapped in relics of blankets, and in one of the outhouses a grim embalmer stood....He dealt with the bodies of high officers only; for, said he—
>
> "I used to be glad to prepare private soldiers. They were wuth a five dollar bill apiece. But, Lord bless you, a Colonel pays a hundred, and a Brigadier-General two hundred. There's lots of them now, and I have cut the acquaintance of everything below a Major. I might," he added, "as a great favor, do a Captain, but he must pay a Major's price. I insist upon that! Such windfalls don't come every day. There won't be another such killing for a century."
>
> —*Campaigns of a Non-Combatant, and His Romaunt Abroad During the War*. George Alfred Townsend. 1866: pp. 180-181.

In 1882, Joseph H. Clarke, a salesman for a coffin company, teamed with Dr. C.M. Lukens of the Pulte Medical College in Cincinnati, to teach embalming. At first they took the classes on the road—an embalming license could be obtained merely by taking a six-day course—but later founded The Clarke School of Embalming, eventually renamed The Cincinnati College of Embalming.

When first introduced, embalming was regarded with some suspicion. Unlike the simple washing and shrouding of the body, it seemed too intrusive. But once adopted, it gave scope for more elaborate funerals and longer times between death and burial. Some old-school undertakers disliked embalming and felt that better results were gotten by icing the corpse. [See ICE-BOX.]

> The preferred mode of preparation of dead bodies is by embalmment. Until very recently, a strong prejudice against touching the sacredness of death existed among the most enlightened people, but fortunately that is wearing away. Soon the custom of using ice—a custom awkward, bungling and shocking—will be entirely dispensed with to make place for an embalmment perfect enough to endure through a long sea voyage.
>
> Since embalming is removing the necessity of speedy burial, the time of interment is also being lengthened. Instead of the second day after death, the fourth or even fifth is now the correct period for burial. This allows more time for friends to arrive and for perfected arrangements.
>
> —*Pittsburgh [PA] Dispatch,* 20 November, 1892: p. 13.

Embalming was also said to give a better appearance to the deceased. And undertakers sometimes implied that embalming was a token of affection for the dear departed.

> The cost of embalming is now reduced to a minimum. Many undertakers will gladly embalm for what they would 'freeze' for, the bother and labor being so much less. Besides, the looks of the subject can be depended on after thorough embalming, while no matter how well it is done frozen subjects cannot be depended on to look well....The average cost where a body is to be shipped to Europe or California is about $50, and then it is guaranteed to keep perfectly. The time is coming in the near future when the body of every one who is loved on earth will be embalmed.
>
> —*The Buffalo [NY] Sunday Morning News,* 8 June, 1884: p. 2.

Embalming was often done at the home of the deceased, rather than at the undertaker's establishment. This called for extreme discretion.

> When I received an order for embalming a body I notified the Doctor, and on an appointed night or morning, taking care that none of the friends of the family should see us enter, we cautiously made our way into the room in which the body lay, then we of course made it known we were in the house. You see the Doctor carried some tools with him in a good-sized satchel. He did not want them to know how much luggage he took in because he would take out just twice as much and that would look suspicious. The first thing done was the cutting of the scalp at the back of the cranium. The scalp was then quickly slit around and all loosened from the skull to the forehead and here it was held or let fall over, so that the hair covered the face; then a small sharp saw was used in taking off the top of the skull; this with the brains and all in the head was placed in a rubber bag provided by the doctor, and after the inside of the head was cleaned thoroughly. He then deposited pieces of cotton saturated with some liquids and other ingredients into the head until it was completely filled and compactly set. The scalp was then drawn back and replaced over the cotton and fastened at the back of the neck, and to all appearance the scalp and hair looked as if they had not been disturbed. Then he next took his knife and opened the abdomen, and after taking out the contents turned up the skin nearly to the lower ribs, where it stayed until he had placed in the same cotton and ingredients to fill up. Next he drew back the skin, sewed it up and gave orders for the remains to be prepared for removal. This completed his work and he left with his rubber bag filled with remains. The body at once resumed a most remarkable appearance, and from that time forward the color was a glowing hue and the features like one calmly reposing in sleep. Of course his charges were high, but his work was decidedly successful and not pleasant to perform.
>
> —*Cincinnati [OH] Enquirer,* 10 December, 1879: p. 2.

Undertakers might do their own embalming or hire a licensed embalmer. There were a number of women embalmers. This was a selling point in undertakers' advertisements, which stressed the propriety of having a lady embalmer to care for women and child clients, a return to the age-old role of women as layers-out of the dead.

> Mr. C.L. Torbett filled a long felt want in Columbus when he secured the services of Miss Fannie D. Gardner, a professional licensed lady undertaker and embalmer, who is now regularly connected with his establishment.
>
> For a number of years there has been a growing desire on the part of everyone to see the time when wife, mother or sister could be prepared for the grave by some gentle, refined woman, instead of having the body embalmed by masculine hands....There are but few if any parents who would not infinitely prefer that their daughters should, in case of death, be dressed and prepared for interment by competent female hands.
>
> —*Columbus [GA] Daily Enquirer,* 25 March, 1900: p. 6.

Women Entering the Gruesome Field
A Prominent and Practical Preserver of the Dead
Talks Interestingly of the Art.

> We have a school right here where we teach embalming, and we've turned out a couple of dozen women embalmers in this city alone, besides those we have sent all over the country. We have a class now which began last week. There was one woman in that. I think she must be sixty years old. A good many trained nurses take the instruction. They've had a good deal of experience in handling bodies, and they think they can make money out of it in connection with their regular work....
>
> [In our course of instruction] we teach the anatomy of the body, and show them how to locate the arteries and veins. When they have been thoroughly instructed in that, we have them observe a skilled embalmer at work, and finally give them cases themselves, to be treated under the direction of the instructor. There is

considerable demand for women embalmers, and they are quite as skillful as men.

—*Star-Gazette* [Elmira, NY], 4 November, 1896: p. 6.

The most common ingredients in embalming fluid were formaldehyde and arsenic, both exceptionally toxic substances. There are a startling number of reports of people drinking the fluid by accident; it was often carelessly stored and readily available during wakes, where it was kept to sprinkle on the corpse.

A Fatal Draught.

That was indeed a sad affliction that occurred recently in a Connecticut town. A dead infant had been prepared for burial, when an undertaker called the mother into the room, and, handing her a cup, informed her that it contained an embalming solution composed of arsenic and other drugs, and directed her to wet a cloth occasionally and lay it over the face of the dead child to preserve its features. He cautioned her that the solution was a deadly poison, and told her to be careful lest the other children in the house should drink the contents. During the conversation the mother placed the cup upon the mantel and accompanied the undertaker to the door. Suddenly a noise in the room attracted their attention, and, turning, they beheld the next eldest child, aged four years, with the cup of poison in its hands, drinking the contents. With a scream the mother sprang to the side of her child, but only to receive from the hands of the little one the cup drained to its very dregs. Picking the child from the floor, the mother tenderly laid her upon the bed and began to use all the means in her power to destroy the effects of the poison. When the doctor arrived the child was suffering most excruciating agony. Remedies were given to counteract the effect of the poison, but it had already been absorbed into the system and the medicines were ineffectual. Ten minutes later the child was a corpse, and two little coffins instead of one were taken to the cemetery.

—*The Cincinnati [OH] Enquirer,* 5 January, 1884: p. 11.

POISON FOR CHAMPAGNE
Thomas Karns Imbibed of Fluid
Intended to Embalm His Father.

Ouray, Colo., Dec. 27. Closely following the sad death of Michael Karns, who was frozen to death, occurs the tragic death of his son, Thomas at 4 a.m. today.

The remains of the elder Karns arrived from Telluride for burial at this city and were at the house of his son, Thomas.

The undertaker had left some embalming fluid, composed of corrosive sublimate and arsenious acid in dilute alcohol at the house, and in the room with the corpse. The poison fluid was in a bottle labeled "Champagne," and although the undertaker had warned the members of the household of the dangerous character of the fluid, Karns must have forgotten the warning or failed to have heard it.

The first the family and watchers knew that he had taken poison was the query from him as to "what that stuff was," and then he said that he had taken two swallows of it and thought it was whisky.

That was 9 p.m. and both Drs. Rowan and Ashley were hurriedly summoned, but their efforts were without benefit to Karns, who died at 4 in the morning.

—*The Topeka [KS] State Journal*, 27 December, 1897: p. 1.

The Last Word

President Abraham Lincoln was the first president to be embalmed. Henry P. Cattell, who had embalmed Lincoln's son Willie, when the child died of typhoid fever in 1862, was called in to assist embalmer Dr. Charles B. Brown and undertaker Frank T. Sands, who accompanied the body aboard the funeral train on its two-week journey to the late President's final resting place in Illinois. Despite Cattell's optimism about the embalming, the 1,654-mile journey took its toll. It was said that Lincoln's face darkened "as if he had been injured by gun-powder," and had to be powdered and painted to cover the discoloration.

F is for Fisk

The cast-iron case

With little glass window

To see the corpse face

The Fisk burial case was a cast-iron coffin invented in 1848 by Almond D. Fisk, a designer of cast-iron stoves, who patented an "air-tight coffin of cast or raised metal" that looked very like a diving suit in its earliest patent sketch. Later versions were modeled to look like draped shrouds.

The Fisk burial case had its origins in a family tragedy. Almond's brother, Dr. William C. Fisk, died 12 April, 1840 in Lafayette County, Mississippi, far from the family grave plot in Chazy, New York. His father, the Rev. Solomon Fisk, was distraught that his son could not be brought back to be buried with his family. This inspired Almond Fisk to create an air-tight coffin so that bodies could be shipped long distances. Fisk's patent contained the further suggestion that "the air may be exhausted so completely as entirely to prevent the decay of the contained body...or...the coffin may be filled with any gas or fluid having the property of preventing putrefaction."

Fisk's coffins proved popular with the rich and elite. Dolley Madison and former Vice President John C. Calhoun were buried in Fisk burial cases. After Fisk's early death at age 32 in 1850, the company was sold several times, eventually becoming Crane & Breed of Cincinnati, Ohio.

Sometimes the Fisk did what it says on the tin: there are reports of bodies shipped long distances arriving in excellent condition. The faces of the dead, unearthed a century after burial, seen through the coffins' plate-glass windows, testify to the Fisk's effectiveness. When the bodies were removed from the old Union Cemetery in Philadelphia in 1857, a curious discovery was made.

> One of the coffins brought to the surface was constructed of solid iron, and of the shape of a torpedo boat, long and pointed at the ends. Upon unscrewing the lid there was found the body of a man in a perfect state of preservation, not the slightest trace of discoloration being apparent, although, according to the records, the interment must have taken place fully a half century ago. The body rested in drapings of the most costly satin, colored and white, and the red hair upon the head, as well as the mustache of the same

color, were as intact as though the burial had taken place but a couple of days before.

This is attributed to the fact that the covering of heavy plate glass beneath the lid rendered the iron casket absolutely air tight.

—*The Topeka [KS] State Journal,* 25 April, 1892: p. 1.

Iron coffins were recommended to prevent the spread of diseases and were also advertised as a deterrent to body snatchers. A sealed iron coffin was more difficult to open and resurrectionists couldn't dig down to the head of an iron coffin, break it open and drag out the corpse by the neck. Their use as a kind of personal, rather than parish, mortsafe [See GLOSSARY] was yet another of the advantages touted for the metallic burial case.

Here is a sampling of puff pieces and advertisements for the Fisk Burial Case:

Important Discovery.

Mr. A.D. Fish, [*sic*] of New York, is exhibiting his patent metallic coffin in the rotunda at the Capitol. He has proofs of his ability to preserve the dead for any desired time or purpose, without decomposition or change of features, and at a very simple and trifling expense. For those who desire the preservation of their deceased friends at a distance from home, or for vaults, or ordinary interment, this promises to be a valuable invention, and worth an examination.

—*The Jeffersonian* [Stroudsburg, PA], 22 March, 1849: p. 2.

"Simple and trifling expense" is, perhaps, subjective. The first coffins made by Almond Fisk weighed over 300 pounds and cost from $50 to $100. At the time a wooden coffin might cost $2.00.

FISK'S METALLIC BURIAL CASKETS AND CASES

Are manufactured of Cast Metal, in imitation of rose-wood, as well finished and as highly polished as the best Rosewood Piano. They are perfectly AIR TIGHT, INDESTRUCTIBLE, and FREE from ENCROACHMENTS of VERMIN or WATER.

We disclaim all connection with the VARIOUS IMITATIONS manufactured of SHEET IRON and other Materials.

W.M. Raymond & Co.
Sole Manufacturers and Proprietors.
MANUFACTORY, NEWTOWN, L.I.
Warerooms and Office, No. 348 PEARL ST., N.Y.

—*Army and Navy Journal and Gazette of the Regular and Volunteer Forces*, 19 November, 1864: p. 207.

The funeral of former First Lady Dolley Madison provided ideal product placement for the Fisk.

Funeral of Mrs. Madison.

The most distinguished honors have been paid to the memory of Mrs. Madison. No mark of respect has been withheld. It was the first occasion on which the metallic air-tight case of Fish [*sic*] & Raymond's patent manufacture has been used in this city for the interment of remains. It is of a different shape from a coffin, and is stripped of the painful associations which usually attend the ordinary receptacle of the dead. The case is metallic. When the lid is put on, it is strongly cemented and made air-tight, and thus the body is preserved to a great degree from the process of decomposition, and does not become disagreeable to the senses. In that part of the lid which is just over the face a small glass is put, which enables the spectator to catch the features; and when it is buried in the ground, the glass is covered with a metallic plate, on which is inscribed the name of the deceased.

—*The Union* [Washington, D.C.], 17 July, 1849: p. 3.

It may not have been disagreeable to the senses, but sometimes the air-tight seal was just *too* perfect.

In 1875 Mr. James A. Watson, of Clover, whose family then resided in Yorkville, lost a child, aged three or four years, by death. At that time Mr. Watson was living in Baltimore...he could not conveniently leave his business to attend the funeral, and in his absence only temporary burial was given the body....The burial case—a Fisk metallic—was raised from the grave, and a natural desire to look upon the face of the child which died and was buried in the father's absence, prompted Mr. Watson to ask Mr. Jeffreys to remove the lid covering the glass panel over the face. The lid was unscrewed and removed...an explosion of gas ensued, shattering the glass, which was a quarter of an inch thick, into numberless fragments, several striking Mr. Watson in the face, cutting it severely. One piece struck the bridge of the nose, cutting entirely through it. A few pieces of the glass also struck Mr. Jeffreys, but he was not seriously hurt. The casket had been out of the ground several minutes when the explosion occurred, which was the result of the expansion by the warmth of the sun of the gas formed in it. The report of the explosion was equal to that of a dynamite cartridge, and was noticed by persons on Main street, more than a quarter of a mile distant.

The face of the child was in excellent preservation, as were also its burial clothes, and a wreath of flowers on the breast seemed to be nearly as fresh as when buried twelve and a half years ago.

—*The Lancaster [PA] Examiner*, 6 January, 1886: p. 2

Cast-iron burial cases even found their way into the joke repertoire.

A patent iron coffin dealer advertises that any one who uses his invention will never use any other.

—*Thames [NZ] Advertiser*, 27 March, 1878: p. 3.

The Last Word

Some other well-preserved bodies found in Fisk burial cases are "The Lady in Red," found in Mississippi in 1869; a little girl, later identified as Edith Howard Cook who was unearthed in 2016 during work on a San Francisco home; and Martha Peterson, a Black woman, who died of smallpox while working as a housekeeper for Almond Fisk's brother-in-law, William Mead Raymond. Her body was discovered in 2011 in Queens, New York.

G is Gates Ajar
In flowers or stone
They swing open wide
To a heavenly home

The design called "Gates Ajar" was one of the most popular funeral flower arrangements of the nineteenth and early twentieth century. These elaborate depictions of open gates were constructed of wire frames filled with wet moss and covered in flowers attached to toothpicks. The image was also found on tombstones.

It would be logical to think that the Gates Ajar were inspired by the "pearly gates" of Heaven imagery, but the motif actually arose out of an 1868 novel by Elizabeth Stuart Phelps, about a woman who loses her faith after her brother is killed in the Civil War. The novel presents a consoling and welcoming view of Heaven where the gates are ajar for all. The image was so popular that large Gates Ajar floral staircases were installed at public parks. The theme was also the basis for a number of poems and songs.

> The most beautiful Gates Ajar I ever saw was entirely of white, with garlands of white roses around the posts. A white dove was so placed as to appear in the darkened room to be taking his flight to heaven with a soul in his charge.
>
> —*Floral Designs*. John Horace McFarland. 1888: pp. 132-141.

Florists created many variations on the theme, some even incorporating cutting-edge technology.

> A novel and quite effective innovation in floral work was seen at a funeral recently. The design consisted of a magnificent "Gates Ajar," over which was the conventional crown surmounted by a cross. The novelty consisted of a tiny electric light which shone like a star on the apex of the cross. The effect was beautiful.
>
> —*The American Florist,* 15 March, 1889: p. 368.

The names of floral tributes and their donors were often listed in accounts of funerals in local newspapers, so there was much incentive to send the most lavish arrangement one could afford.

It would be interesting to know who the United States senators are who have united to send to General Sheridan's funeral, through a Boston florist, a "floral piece" which is thus described:

The piece is nearly six feet high, six feet long and four feet in width, and represents Gates Ajar. In the centre are two large pillars, from which are hung two gates. Joining the pillars is an arch, having in the centre a cross and crown. Suspended from the arch is a pure white dove, and on the top of each pillar is a large star. Looking through the open gate and picket fence is a representation of the garden of Eden, in which flowers, roses and ferns abound in artistic profusion. On the right corner is a beautiful bouquet of roses tied with satin ribbon. Across the front is the inscription, "Light lie the earth on thee."

—*Boston [MA] Evening Transcript,* 8 August, 1888: p. 4.

The imagery was used in the most pathetic of stories.

Gates Ajar.

The death of a well-known gentleman had called forth many expressions of sympathy from friends, in the way of a profusion of flowers, in beautiful designs. After they had been placed around him as he lay in the casket, his little daughter, Alice, of 4 years, was led by her mamma into the room to look upon the face of her dead papa. She was naturally attracted by the flowers, and by the design of "The Gates Ajar." Her mamma told her that "the beautiful gate" had opened, and papa had passed through and would never come back to them again. The child looked steadily at her papa's face for a few moments, then climbed up so she could reach over and kiss his cold lips, saying: "Papa, dear, speak to me and say you will come to 'the beautiful gate' and meet your little Alice some day."

—*The Weekly Detroit [MI] Free Press,* 23 January, 1886: p. 2.

"Gates Ajar" is also seen in jokes as shorthand for death or a funeral.

HONK! HONK!
Railroad crossing,
Speeding car,
Fragments tossing,
Gates ajar!

—*Grey River [Greymouth, NZ] Argus,* 2 June, 1916: p. 5.

The author of *Gates Ajar*, Elizabeth Stuart Phelps, was both amused and appalled at the popularity of her creation.

> There was a "Gates Ajar" tippet for sale in the country groceries; I have fancied that it was a knit affair of as many colors as the jewels in the eternal portals, and extremely openwork. There was a "Gates Ajar" collar—paper, I fear—loading the city counters. Ghastly rumors have reached me of the existence of a "Gates Ajar" cigar. I have never personally set my eyes upon these tangible forms of earthly fame. If the truth must be told, I have kept a cowardly distance from them....Then there was, and still exists, the "Gates Ajar" funeral piece. This used to seem to me the least serious of them all; but...when I saw...how many mourning people were so constituted as to find comfort in it, I came to have a tolerance for it which even grows into a certain tenderness. I may frankly admit that I have begun to love it since I heard about the two ragged little newsboys who came to the eminent city florist, with all their savings clenched in their grimy fists, and thus made known their case:
>
> "Ye see, Larks he was our pardner—him an' us sold on the same beat—an' he jes' got run over by a 'lectric, and it went over his back, so they tuk him to the horspittle, 'n Larks he up an' died there yestiddy. So us fellars were goin' to give Larks a stylish funeril, you bet. We liked Larks—an'...there ain't nothin' mean 'bout us, come to buryin' of Larks; 'n we've voted to settle on one them Gates Ajar pieces—made o' flowers, doncherknow. So me 'n him an' the other fellars we've saved up all our propurty...an' here it is, mister. I told the kids ef there was more 'n enough you's trow in a

few greens, anyhow. Make up de order right away, mister, and give us our money's worf now, sure—for Larks."

The gamin proudly counted out upon the marble slab of that fashionable flower store the sum of seventy-five cents. The florist—blessings on him!—is said not to have undeceived the little fellows, but to have duly honored their "order;" and the biggest and most costly Gates Ajar piece to be had in the market went to the hospital, and helped to bury Larks.

—*Chapters From a Life*. Elizabeth Stuart Phelps. 1896: pp. 114-115.

THE LAST WORD

A large, dried Gates Ajar arrangement for President Grant's funeral still exists at Ulysses S. Grant Cottage National Historic Landmark, Gansevoort, New York.

H is for Hearse
Vehicle of gloom
A funereal float
With crape, drape, and plume

The hearse—the last ride—was, in many funerals, the dramatic vehicle to carry the corpse to the cemetery. Hearses gleamed with silver fittings and glossy paint, and might be topped with carved urns and angels or fountains of plumes. Some hearses had glass windows, draped with curtains, while others had window draperies carved on wooden side and door panels. In cold climates, hearses could be adapted for winter funerals by having their wheels replaced with sleigh runners.

The hearse was the centerpiece of the funeral procession. Hearse-proud undertakers boasted of new hearses and how much they had cost.

> Mr Mold, the undertaker, was a hustler. In his opinion even a funeral could be made a thing of beauty, if not a joy forever. He stood on the kerb surveying with much pride a glorious motor hearse, his latest innovation.
>
> "What do you think of it—pretty smart, eh?" he asked a friend.
>
> "Splendid, old man; people will be simply dying to ride in it!"
>
> —*The North-Eastern Daily Gazette*
> [Middlesbrough, Cleveland, England], 22 September, 1909: p. 4.

Ostrich feather plumes, displayed on hearse and horses, were thought to be the proper funereal display, although they were criticized as vulgar by funeral reformers.

> The subject of the hearse must not be left without some mention of the funeral plumes. In those districts where this "luxury" can least be afforded, and where its appearance is, if only for this reason, the more incongruous, the sable plumes of death are sometimes seen.
>
> The roof of the hearse is covered with a forest of these forbidding ornaments and a sort of sweep's brush nods from the horses' heads—white in the case of the burial of a child. Thus do the uninformed love to do honour to their dead.
>
> —*Funeral Customs: Their Origin and Development*,
> Bertram S. Puckle, 1926: pp. 127-128.

Royal and state funerals brought out the most elaborate of hearses. Although Queen Victoria's coffin was drawn on a simple gun carriage, no expense was spared when designing the funeral car for the venerable military hero and politician, the Duke of Wellington, in 1852. The plans for this massive hearse, which was cast from bronze cannons captured at the Battle of Waterloo and covered in a canopy of embroidered Indian fabric, were approved by Albert, the Prince Consort, who lauded the vehicle as a triumph of English ingenuity and craftsmanship.

The Times described the lavishly ornamented funeral car:

> The whole lower part is of bronze, supported by six wheels. Above this metallic frame work rises a rich pediment of gilding, in the panels of which the...list of victories is inscribed....On the sides of this pediment were arranged lofty trophies of arms, including spears, muskets, bayonets, swords and flags and surmounted by the Duke's coronets and batons. A similar trophy stood in front....Over the bier and its bearers, the gilded handles of which protruded from beneath, was arranged the sumptuous velvet pall, powdered with silver and showing the legend round it, "Blessed are the dead that die in the Lord," and terminated by a magnificent fringe of silver two feet deep. The coffin with the Duke's hat and sword resting on it, surmounted the bier, and from four great halberds rising at each corner was suspended a magnificent canopy, with pendant cords and tassels of the richest and most costly description. This gigantic vehicle was 27 feet long, 10 feet broad, 17 feet high and weighing from 10-11 tons. Twelve of the largest and finest black horses were harnessed with velvet housings having the arms of the deceased splendidly embroidered on them, and with heads surmounted by nodding plumes, they looked quite elephantine.
>
> —*The Times* [London, England], 19 November, 1852: p. 5.

Some critics were less than impressed by the funeral car. Thomas Carlyle wrote that it was an "incoherent muddle of expensive palls, flags, sheets and poles...more like one of the street carts that hawk doormats than a bier for a hero." It was described as "that hideous article of upholstery" in Parliament. The hearse was eventually put on display in the crypt of St. Paul's Cathedral and may now be seen at Stratfield Saye House, Wellington's country mansion.

Like biers, hearses originally were owned by a village or parish and used to carry the local dead to their graves. They were stored in the parish or county "hearse house," which sometimes doubled as a morgue. Later, undertakers purchased hearses to lease to their clients.

In the United States, until the advent of the automobile hearse, a smart team of plumed hearse horses were a cherished commodity, well-known and sometimes beloved by the communities they served. The acquisition of a new pair of hearse horses was, like the purchase of a new hearse, an important event—something to be puffed in the papers.

As late as 1911, E.F. Parks, an undertaker in Bryan, Texas, announced the arrival of "our fine team of hearse horses," rhapsodizing:

> "They are simply beautiful. White with a touch of red about the ears, back and hip. They are full brothers 5 and 6 years old."
>
> —*The Bryan [TX] Eagle,* 16 March, 1911: p. 1.

Undertaker Parks even ran a contest for several weeks in the local newspaper to name the horses, selecting "Prince" and "Pilot" as the winning names.

Black Belgian stallions were the most prized hearse horses, although white horses were often used for the funerals of children and the unmarried. In England, a matched set of black Drenthe horses from Hanover were employed at royal funerals. If dark-coated hearse horses had any lighter hairs, the light patches would be painted to match. Some of the cheaper imported stallions lacked the all-important tail-weepers and were provided with false tails:

> A queer English custom is that of decorating the black hearse horses with long false black tails. They attract no more notice on a street in Liverpool than do the black nets used in this country to cover the horses.
>
> —*Pierre [SD] Weekly Free Press,* 16 November, 1905: p. 1.

Street-car or trolley hearses were popular, particularly in Mexico and South America. The first electric, motorized hearses were introduced to Britain in the 1890s; they were first used in the United States in the early 1900s. Some were made from a traditional hearse body mounted on an automobile chassis.

> A firm of undertakers in Fresno, California, has introduced an electric hearse, which rejoices in the title of an "auto-morgue-mobile."
>
> —*The Bath Chronicle* [Bath, Avon, England], 15 March, 1906: p. 3.

> **HEARSE IS OUT OF DATE.**
>
> Man's last earthly ride has undergone some style changes in recent years. The ornate hearse is out of date and most citizens now go to their final rest in a vehicle not greatly different from the family automobile.
>
> One of the country's largest hearse makers, located in Quincy, manufacture a plain coach resembling a limousine, but with the door in the rear....
>
> The horse-drawn hearse was discarded about fifteen years ago. The hearse manufacturers build the bodies and mount them on various makes of automobiles.
>
> —*The La Belle [MO] Star,* 6 November, 1925: p. 2.

As with any new technology, there were naysayers. Many thought the speed of the motor hearse was disrespectful when compared with the dignified pace of a horse-drawn funeral.

> "We don't want to hurry to the cemetery," is the universal remark of those who object to the motor hearse.
>
> —*The Topeka [KS] Daily Capital,* 6 July, 1915: p. 6.

The Last Word

Originally, the word "hearse" had nothing to do with the vehicle. Until about 1650, according to the *Oxford English Dictionary*, the hearse was a cage-like candle holder that was placed on a coffin or a tomb.

I is for ice box
It freezes the clay
It ices the loved one
For family display

For many decades, in the days before refrigeration, the ice box was the best method of preserving a corpse until it could be buried. Many styles of ice box were patented. They were called "corpse-preservers," "ice-boxes," and "corpse coolers." One brand was known as the "Fresh-ever." Some were human-sized ice-chests; others were meant to fit over the torso to delay intestinal decomposition. In 1869 Milwaukee, undertakers charged $3 to $5 a day for ice box rentals. In 1885, the use of an ice box for a New York funeral cost $15.00.

Some undertakers iced the corpse until it was nearly frozen solid and then let it thaw. The ice box would be equipped with a handy hose to hang out the window or into a nearby bucket. The sound and smell of the water running off the thawing corpse is one of the lost sensory experiences of the nineteenth century.

> In cases where the body is to be kept for some days before the family assembles for the funeral, or where the disease has been such as to render all deodorizers and disinfectants powerless, the body is put into a "corpse preserver," which is a coffin with double sides, the inner one being of sheet-iron, and constructed on the same principle as the vases used for icing champagne. The corpse is thus practically frozen, and can be preserved for almost any length of time, an aperture in the top being left to show the face of the deceased....This is a thoroughly American arrangement, and one in perfect harmony with the prevalent taste for ice and everything iced in this country.
>
> —*Richwood [OH] Gazette,* 14 January, 1875: p. 4.

> [T]he undertaker brought a rectangular box, two by seven feet and about six inches deep, into which the body was laid and ice packed around and on it. The water was drained from the box by a small spout into a bucket that stood on the floor. Still later the ice-box was coffin-shaped, about six and a half feet long, thirty inches wide at the shoulder and twenty-four inches deep. The sight of that box caused many a shudder. The body, wrapped in a sheet, was laid into the bottom of the box, and a metal tray filled with

cracked ice and resting on catches in the box was placed over it, and a close fitting lid was shut down tight. A small spout carried the water from this refrigerator.

—*A History of Catasauqua in Lehigh County, Pennsylvania.* James Franklin Lambert and Henry J. Reinhard. 1914: p. 364.

While arterial embalming had been popular since the Civil War, some conservative undertakers, perhaps cautious about the toxic chemicals involved, shunned embalming, believing that they got better, more natural results by the older method of icing the corpse.

"Before the patent ice boxes were in use," continued Mr. William, "I was called on to bury a young man whose death was caused by drowning. It was in warm weather, and the family desired that the funeral should be put off a few days. The bath tub was used, and he was laid in it, covered with ice, and kept splendidly. In fact, he looked so much better in death than he did in life that his mother could not be made to believe that life was extinct, and for this reason the hour of the funeral services was twice postponed until her family physician arrived and made an examination.

—*Arkansas City [KS] Daily Traveler,* 12 July, 1888: p. 6.

The public also was uneasy about embalming and slow to give up the ice box. A Philadelphia undertaker noted class divisions in the use of ice:

I embalm whenever people will let me. A good many object, however, especially among the lower classes, to having the body touched with the knife. They're not content unless I come at them with a big box and 150 pounds of ice.

—*The Philadelphia [PA] Times,* 19 August, 1883: p. 5.

Some doctors criticized the icing of corpses, claiming that unconscious persons might be frozen to death if they were mistaken for dead.

The morbid dread of being buried alive that is entertained by some nervous people, is entirely groundless. Such a thing is practically impossible, for the simple reason that a person supposed to be a corpse, but not really such, would inevitably be frozen to death in the ice box long before the funeral.

—*The Cincinnati [OH] Enquirer,* 21 June, 1896: p. 25.

This highly dramatic incident was related by an undertaker of the anti-ice-box school.

No body should ever be placed on ice unless it is rigid in the extreme. Only a few days ago a very striking instance came to my notice through a friend of mine, who was in the undertaking business. He had a call to prepare a lady for burial up town. He went to the house with his assistants, and, after properly laying her out, dressed her in nice robes and placed the body in a rich casket....The next day...a number of the deceased lady's friends came to witness the sad rites over the dead....At the conclusion of the service all passed around the casket to take their parting look. The undertaker stood at the head of the receptacle ready to close it for the grave, when a lady moved silently to the corpse, and, after gazing on the features of the dead, suddenly drew back and whispered to the astonished undertaker. "Did you notice her eyes? I think I saw them move." The undertaker could not realize such a thing, and, without answering directly, said: "You must be mistaken, madam. Mrs. ___ has been dead for nearly two days."

"But see! Look at her eyelids, they are twitching; I am sure they move. See!" exclaimed the lady again as she pointed at the eyes of the corpse.

The undertaker now looked down on the face of the dead, and started back as he really did notice the eyelids slightly twitch....

At this he...called one of his assistants, whom he told to immediately send away the hearse and coaches and hastily go for a physician.

The body was taken out from the casket and placed upon a couch, and restoratives quickly applied, and before half an hour had elapsed respiration returned, and the lady returned to life. The undertaker had the empty casket taken back to his store, and the floral tributes were preserved for the family....

This same undertaker a few months ago, before he left business, was called to a house where a lady had just died. As soon as he entered he said the body must be placed on ice at once. One of the ladies, however, stepped forward and said: "No, sir; you will not put that body on ice."

"Why not?" asked the man in surprise.

"Because she might be yet alive for all we know, and if you put her on ice before at least decomposition shows itself, you might keep her dead anyway."

"That's impossible, my dear woman; do you not see the lady is dead?"

"No, sir," quietly retorted the lady; "she only looks dead, as I did once, and is in just the same position, and you know it, too."

The undertaker looked at the woman....

It was the same lady whom he was to bury some time ago, but came to life, leaving the casket and arrangements on his hands.

—*The Cincinnati [OH] Enquirer* 16 February 1881: p. 2

The Last Word

Corpses were sometimes iced for shipment, a practice which provided fodder for the humorists:

It was on a railway run in North-West America; the thermometer was 120 deg. in the shade.

For some two hours the only sound that broke the rhythmic throbbing of the train was:

"Waiter! Ice!"

"Yessir; coming sir," responded that individual.

For about that period the supply of ice was sufficient for the demand, but at length, in response to a particularly irate traveller's demand for further coolers, came the laconic reply:

"Really gentlemen, I don't think I dare bring you any more ice. If I do the corpse won't keep till the end of the journey!"

—*Evening Post* [Wellington, NZ], 25 October, 1902: p. 10.

J is for jet

A jewel most doleful

Of mournful appearance

And color most coal-ful

How did a type of coal become a fashionable symbol of Victorian death and an accessory treasured by modern-day Goths?

Jet, a type of coal called lignite, is fossilized wood, which was subjected to pressure over millions of years. It had a dull appearance before being polished, which made it ideal for mourning jewelry, although it was also carved into souvenir and sentimental jewelry. In England, the Victorian center of jet mining and production was Whitby, in North Yorkshire, a seaside town where lumps of jet still wash up on the shore.

Jet worn for mourning was mentioned as early as the seventeenth century. It was specified for court mourning for Princess Charlotte of Wales, at her death in 1817, for Queen Charlotte, who died late in 1818, and King George IV's death in 1830. Queen Victoria wore Whitby jet to mourn Prince Albert and her preference solidified its status as *the* mourning gemstone.

> Jet is always fashionable, it being, we may say, the only ornament permissible in mourning.
>
> —*Myra's Journal of Dress and Fashion,* April, 1877: p. 6.

> **JET JEWELRY.**
>
> Jet jewelry is much in vogue this season, both in and out of mourning. The French jet is made of glass, and the English jet of carbon; the latter is more durable, though not quite so pretty....Necklaces, with medallion or other pendants, cost from $7 to $30; wide bracelets from $7 to $25; and brooch and ear-rings from $5 to $30.
>
> —*Harper's Bazaar,* 8 January, 1870: p. 19.

Just as Peter Robinson's Mourning Emporium stood ready to travel with dressmakers and mourning goods to the homes of the bereaved at a moment's notice, the Whitby jet merchants were eager to dispatch their wares on approval.

> The late Queen Victoria was a great admirer of jet, and during her reign Whitby flourished from the industry as never before. Muff chains, lockets, penholders, cigarette holders, bookmarks, shirt

studs, cuff links, hat pins, spangles and bangles, flowers, and medallions were produced in great quantities and were shipped all over Europe and especially over the British empire. When any person of importance died in any part of Europe the Whitby merchants would immediately send a box of jet mourning by express to the bereaved family. Such jewelry as was kept was paid for by check, and the rest of the stock returned.

—*Our Paper* [Concord Junction, MA], 12 December, 1903: p. 796.

"Dull" is the adjective most often paired with the word "jet" in the fashion columns.

> Jet is now so fashionable that it has helped immensely in making a variety as to watch chains, lorgnette chains, &c., but only dull jet should be worn with the first mourning. The dull jet spangled gowns or crape gowns trimmed with jet for dinner wear are about the most becoming that a woman puts on.
>
> —*Idaho Statesman* [Boise, ID], 14 June, 1903: p. 3.

> When jet is worn [for court mourning] it must be dull, and not the bright French jet that is so generally worn on other occasions.
>
> —*The Bystander: An Illustrated Weekly Devoted to Travel,* 18 May, 1910: p. 326.

The immense demand for jet led to the creation of imitations such as vulcanite (vulcanized rubber), bog oak (trees preserved in peat bogs), gutta percha (latex from a Malaysian tree) and the so-called "French jet," or black glass, which often has a very sharp-edged, Gothic aesthetic. How black glass came to be called "French Jet" is a mystery. The term first appears in the early 1840s.

Nineteenth-century sources do not give any clues about the name's origin. Modern publications offer various theories, such as the French were early manufacturers of black glass or copied real jet mourning jewelry in glass. It has also been suggested that the glass was made in Bohemia and shipped to France and England to be made into jewelry and accessories. Lou Taylor, in *Mourning Dress*, writes that black glass "was called 'French jet', probably to give it some allure." The phrase also had the effect of profitably obscuring the material's origins. Anything labeled "French" was highly fashionable and French mourning goods were doubly desirable since the French "excelled at the *funèbre*."

There was a constant rivalry in the marketplace between genuine jet and French Jet. Jay's Mourning Emporium, in 1888, impartially advertised French Jet and "Real Whitby Jet."

> Much of what is called mourning jewellery is made of "French jet." To the lay eye it looks like black glass, finely faceted and mounted on a metal foundation, but I have heard a shopman speak of it as garnet. The hue is as ebon as that of Whitby jet; but it is much more effective, and can be more artistically wrought. Really good specimens are sufficiently costly to satisfy those who dislike "cheap handsomenesse."
>
> —*Notes and Queries* 8th Series, 31 March, 1894: p. 255.

> Mr. Langdale [of Standard Jetworks, Baxtergate, Whitby] has also broken fresh ground by taking up the manufacture of all kinds of millinery, dress and mantle ornaments, buttons, buckles, fancy pins, hat and hair ornaments, floral sprays, &c. In this department he is a pioneer, showing a splendid assortment of new and suitable designs, which are calculated to appeal to the tastes of the better classes, and thus to bring in real Whitby jet goods as a substitute for the black glass imitations that flood the market under the name of French jet. Nothing in the shape of black jewellery or ornaments can for a moment compare with genuine Whitby hard jet in lustre, durability, and unchanging colour. Moreover, this famous material is much lighter than any kind of foreign jet or glass imitation, and is capable of being wrought in designs far more elegant and beautiful.
>
> —*Progress, Commerce*, 1893: p. 229.

During the first World War, heavy mourning was discouraged as bad for morale. It was suggested that the "old-fashioned jet brooch" replace crape as a symbol of bereavement.

> When the question was being discussed the other day in a room full of women, knitting for the Red Cross, one sweet-faced little woman pointed to a beautiful old-fashioned jet brooch at her throat. "This," said she, "is my mourning. It is a treasured family heirloom full of dear associations. The members of our family do not believe in mourning apparel, but this brooch represents to me, mourning. It is never worn except at such periods, and is then worn constantly—with all costumes. When I wear this brooch, I am in mourning as truly as though clothed in deepest black...."
>
> —*Oregonian* [Portland, OR], 23 June, 1918: p. 73.

By the 1920s, jet had largely fallen from favor for mourning.

> If these mortuary jewels were as a whole very ugly, what shall be said of the hideous lumps of crudely manufactured jet which it is still considered by some classes of society to be necessary to wear when "in mourning," or the even more preposterous "half-mourning" sets of ear-rings and the like, in which a little silver is introduced to lighten the effect. Whitby, which for centuries has been the seat of the jet industry, still carries on a trade on [*sic*] these ghoulish appendages impervious alike to enlightenment or ridicule.
>
> —*Funeral Customs: Their Origin and Development*, Bertram S. Puckle. 1926: pp. 270-271.

The Last Word

How to tell the difference between jet and French jet: jet is warm; glass is cold. Jet is soft; glass is hard. Jet is also lighter and less brittle than glass.

K is for keen

A funereal wail

From banshee or mourner

It makes the heart quail

The tradition of wailing and lamenting for a death is found all over the world. During the Victorian era, it was particularly noted in Ireland where cries and exclamations of sorrow were paired with tributes to the virtues of the deceased and questions such as "how could you leave us?" This was called keening, from the Irish term "caoineadh," "to cry," a practice of great antiquity, going back to at least the twelfth century and perhaps earlier. A keener, who was always female—the *bean chaointe*—might be a relative, neighbor, or a hired professional. She keened at the wake and while following the coffin to the grave.

> The dramatic effect of the scene is very powerful; the darkness of the death-chamber, illumined only by candles that glare upon the corpse—the manner of repetition or acknowledgment that runs round when the keener gives out a sentence—the deep, yet suppressed sobs of the nearer relatives—and the stormy, uncontrollable cry of the widow or bereaved husband, when allusion is made to the domestic virtues of the deceased,—all heighten the effect of the keen; but in the open air, winding round some mountain pass, when a priest, or person greatly beloved and respected, is carried to the grave, and the keen, swelled by a thousand voices, is borne upon the mountain echoes—it is then absolutely magnificent....
>
> This keen is very ancient, and there is a tradition that its origin is supernatural, as it is said to have been first sung by a chorus of invisible spirits in the air over the grave of one of the early kings of Ireland....It is altogether extemporaneous; and it is sometimes astonishing to observe with what facility the keener will put the verses together, and shape her poetical images to the case of the person before her.
>
> —*Ballou's Dollar Monthly Magazine*, January, 1860: p. 12.

The English, more reticent in their mourning practices, always remarked on the "wild" nature of Irish keening.

> I once met a funeral procession in its passage from the town of Killarney to Mucruss abbey, which exhibited a remarkable instance of apparent vehemence of grief, and real indifference. The coffin

> was placed in a small hearse under a canopy, and upon it was seated an old gray-headed woman, who seemed to be actually convulsed with sorrow. She uttered the most doleful cries; alternately smote her breast and the lid of the coffin; and occasionally prostrating herself upon it, endeavoured as it were to embrace the once beloved object of her affections....I was irresistibly led to mix among the train; when, to my great surprise, I found that she had not shed a single tear. After a few minutes her clamour was suspended, and she turned to speak with indifference to the people near her....I was not able to learn, whether she was one of those persons common at Killarney, who are hired to attend funerals and to sing the death song; but very probably she was.
>
> The death song, or death cry as it...is most commonly called, is there kept up, incessantly, for several days and nights in the house of the deceased: those women who have the best lungs, and the most lively imagination, get the most money for their services....
>
> —*Illustrations of the Scenery of Killarney and the Surrounding Country*. Isaac Weld. 1807: pp. 26-27.

An American adventurer and travel writer wrote of hearing the keening on Achill Island.

> As we near the remotest part of the island, where the mountains raise their heads in solemn grandeur there are no signs of human habitation except one lonely cottage. Its door is open, but there is no evidence of life. Suddenly the air shivers with the weirdest, loneliest wail I had ever listened to—a sustained, penetrating wail, rising and falling on the sad air, and then shuddering away into silence, rendered all the sadder by the fast approaching shadows of the night. It is the famous "keening" or mourning for the dead. There are professional keeners, and when one is informed of a death she starts for the house of sorrow and commences this melancholy cry as she goes. All the way over hill and dale, by these dark pools and through the bog-pathway, she goes, her cry bringing the women and the children to the doors of all the huts. As she approaches the dead the cry dies away and ceases as she enters the

cottage. Walking round the bier she commences anew and passing outward and away fills all the silence of the deepening night with her melancholy plaint. To hear it any place in Ireland is sad enough, to hear it amidst the desolation of Achill is almost terrifying and never to be forgotten. To-night it sounds like the voices of lost souls from the depths of the dark Atlantic.

—*Wanderings in Ireland.* Michael Myers Shoemaker. 1908: pp. 55-56.

Young Brigid Farrell died in 1935; the keening for her was remembered sixty years later:

> Mrs Malone, Meedin, Tyrellspass remembers a funeral coming to Castletown Geoghegan from Garhy - Brigid Farrell R.I.P. She died young and all the school children went in the funeral procession. As the coffin was been [*sic*] taken out a number of old women twelve to twenty raised the caoine, forming fours across the road and marched across the road after the coffin keening all the way one half the women, one verse, then the other, the next half verse on a note a little higher, you couldn't think of any thing to sound so sorrowful and never disisted [*sic*] till she was laid in the grave.

—Dúchas.ie The Schools' Collection, Volume 0733, Page 084.
https://www.duchas.ie/en/cbes/5009070/4983653/5117076.
(Accessed 5 June, 2023.)

Keening in Ireland died out in the nineteenth century, at least partially due to pressure from the Catholic Church, which regarded the practice as pagan and regressive. Accounts of wakes in Irish communities in the United States only rarely describe keening. This reminiscence, which compares wakes in Ireland with those in St. Louis, is one of the few mentions of keening as practiced in the States.

> I remember...the wakes we had in Connemara 40 years ago....The relatives near the head of the dead and the keener, the old woman that sings the lamentation for the deceased, was at the head on the other side, sitting where she could look into the face of the dead. Keeners could be hired, you know, if there was nobody in

the family could cry the keen. When the room was full, with the visitors sitting on benches, boxes or kishes of turf, pretty soon you'd hear the 'u lu lu' of the keener, a piercing mournful wail and there she'd go on to tell what a good man he was and how happy he met death, and the grief it brought to his people, and she'd pray that he was with the angels and that the winds'd blow soft and the turf grow green over, closing the cry with 'Uhla-uhla-gohla-goane,' which means that he's gone forever and ever. We've had keening in this country, but nothing like the keeners at home....

In this country...when I first came to St. Louis, thirty years ago, there was more freedom at wakes and less respect for the dead than ever I saw in Ireland....There was the same story-telling and singing and all the accompaniments of the old country wake. Often, too, we had the keen cried. I heard it as late as a few years ago, but never since then.

The old-fashioned Irish wake began to die out in St. Louis, and everywhere else, I guess, about ten years ago. One of them is very rare now, very rare, indeed.

—*St. Louis [MO] Post-Dispatch,* 31 July, 1883: p. 5.

The Last Word

There are some who say that the keening at old Irish funerals inspired the legend of the *bean sí* or banshee. Others say that it was the other way round: that it is keeners who imitate the banshee's wail. There are also hints in Irish folklore that a keener might return after death as a banshee.

Since some of the names used for the supernatural death-messenger imply she is a keening woman, and that keening and wailing are among her most prominent traits, it is hardly surprising the idea should have arisen that she was a human keening woman who must continue her activity after death, perhaps because of some neglect or defect in her fulfilment of her duties in this life.

—*The Banshee: The Irish Death-Messenger.*
Patricia Lysaght. 1997: p. 49.

L is for Lychgate

A gate and a bier

A rest for pallbearers

Till Vicar is here

The lychgate was literally a gate between the land of the living and the land of the dead. Lychgate—the name comes from the Anglo-Saxon "lych," a corpse—refers to a roofed structure at the entrance to an English churchyard, marking the boundary between unconsecrated and consecrated ground. It was the gate through which the dead were carried or wheeled to burial and might have a bench or "lych stone" where the bearers of a coffin could set down their burden until the clergyman arrived to begin the first part of the burial service, before proceeding into the church or directly to the grave.

> When the train reaches the churchyard-gate, it halts, and if the clergyman be not ready to receive it, the coffin is sometimes set down upon trestles or chairs, and the company waits till the clergyman appears. It seems to be looked upon as an established mark of respect for the clergyman to meet the funeral at the gate, and it is beautiful to see the serious and unhurried manner in which the country clergyman of the more pure and primitive districts goes forth to receive the dead to its resting-place, repeating aloud as he precedes the funeral to the church, a portion of the service for the occasion.
>
> —*The Rural Life of England*, William Howitt, 1844: p. 588.

Lychgates might be constructed of wood, stone, or brick, with either thatched or tile roofs. The structures were dedicated with religious services and were sometimes erected in memory of a former clergyman. After the First World War, many lychgates were created as war memorials.

> [The lych gate] was a building...gothic in design, with gable windows and side aisles. The floor was fine gravel, and the space was sufficient to accommodate an ordinary funeral company standing....As a rule hearses were not admitted, the coffin being placed on a wheeled bier which was run into the lych gate. The doors being closed the service proceeded in comparative comfort, and at its conclusion the inner gate was opened and the bier...was easily moved by the pall-bearers to the grave side.
>
> —*Southland Times* [Invercargill, NZ], 3 August, 1892: p. 3.

Lychgates were also the focus of local beliefs and superstitions.

> It is considered unlucky for a wedding party to meet a funeral....No bridal pair would under any conditions pass through the lych-gate.
>
> —*Lore and Legend of the English Church.*
> George Smith Tyack. 1899: p. 67.

> In days gone by, the lich-gate was often the scene of a curious superstition...the idea being that the spirit of the last person watches round the churchyard till another is buried, to whom he delivers his charge....[T]errific fights have taken place, at the entrance of the churchyard, to decide which corpse should be buried first.
>
> —*Church Lore Gleanings.* T.F. Thiselton Dyer. 1892: p. 156.

> Another curious superstition is that the churchyard-gate (the Lych-gate) must on no account be made to open outwards—otherwise the spirits of the dead would pass out, and trouble the land. It must open inwards, and the dead must be carried in feet forwards.
>
> —*From the Hebrides to the Himalayas.*
> Constance Frederica Gordon Cumming. 1876, p. 211.

By the 1920s, lychgates were rarely used for their original purpose and it is amusing to find this comment in a gardening book from 1926:

> Why the Lych Gate should always suggest a graveyard to so many people, I really do not know....We hardly realise it, but the Lych Gate is the earliest idea of a summer-house....The Lych Gate of to-day is looked upon as a mere appendage of the churchyard, when in very truth it is one of the finest garden features that we have.
>
> —*Garden Architecture.*
> Thomas Geoffrey Wall Henslow. 1926: pp. 158-159.

The Last Word

Lychgate was spelled in a variety of ways and had several other names: lichgate, lycugate, lyke-gate or as two separate words: lych gate, also wych gate, or resurrection gate.

M is for Mute
Hired to mourn
Dressed all in black
And looking forlorn

While wailing mourners were common in some funeral traditions, the mutes, by contrast, stood silent, stifled by simulated sorrow.

Mutes were paid mourners. These men or children, dressed in black, stood outside a house in mourning with draped staffs that looked like crape-covered brooms. Mutes always looked mournful; some even cried on cue. They might also walk in a funeral procession.

This grave profession arose in England from the many household attendants at early aristocratic funerals. Some of these carried draped staffs—or staves of office, indicating their rank—as a sign of mourning for their late lord. Eventually the custom was copied by middle- and lower-class mourners, even as the nobility abandoned it.

Mutes might be an undertaker's employees, paupers from the workhouse, or just men hired off the street. Mutes were often described as having "red noses." They had a reputation as drunkards because they were stationed outside in all weathers and usually were treated to gin or something equally warming at intervals. Their drinking and ability to cry on cue were noted severely by authors and journalists. While the practice never caught on in the United States, the American press had much to say about mutes and English funerals.

> If we should not at first be sure of death, the presence on the doorsteps of two lugubrious persons would prove it. These, relieved with other two at certain intervals, stand one on each side the door to weep until the period shall be ended between the death and the removal to the cemetery. These paid mourners are "mutes." Their business is to weep, and they perform it faithfully. In solemn black garments, hands in black gloves, broad streamers of crape, called "weepers," about their hats, they ply handkerchiefs to their eyes, black bordered and gloomy. When there are no passers by they discuss the local politics or their own affairs. Directly some one heaves in sight up go the handkerchiefs. The ends of their noses are suspiciously red. One feels that gin is the cause of such a perpetual flow of salt water from their weak, reddish eyes.
>
> —*The Wichita [KS] Eagle,* 6 August, 1887: p. 7.

Passing along a street, your attention is attracted to two dismal looking men standing at the door of a house. They are dressed in very deep mourning. They wear long, black cloth cloaks, and their hats are completely enveloped in crape, the ends of which hangs a yard or more down their backs. Each holds a staff, around the top of which is rolled a large bundle of crape. These men are called mutes. They are heart-broken looking creatures; long practice has given them their rueful expression, and their wages depend on the amount of sorrow they are able to *look*....

—*Salem [MA] Observer,* 17 May, 1851: p. 1.

Those who employed mutes paid handsomely for that essential, correct degree of grief.

My master's face was an epitome of grief, but nothing to mine; so he engaged me right off to be a "mute," which all the world knows is to stand at the door for an hour before the funeral starts, with a thing like a cripple's crutch covered with black silk, and tied round the waist with a white sash. My master had a regular tariff of grief from five pounds to fifty, I seldom appeared except abject misery at ten pounds was required. My master appreciated me, and I got an easy living out of death, and enjoyed life in a cheerful cemetery sort of way....if you want an easy living, and have a woeful countenance, be a jolly mute."

—*The Colonist* [Nelson, NZ], 21 December, 1892: p. 3.

The Parisian funeral mute was known as the *Croque-mort*. This funereal functionary took his job very seriously, organizing protests and strikes when aggrieved about working conditions. The *Croque-morts* even had their own trade publication.

For the Funeral Mutes.

Paris. The latest thing in humorous papers in Paris is "Le Petit Corbillard" [*Le Petit corbillard illustré*](The Little Hearse), an illustrated fortnightly paper costing three-halfpence, and containing more or less humorous articles and pictures about funerals and everything that interests the funeral mute. Among other things there is an epitaph competition, and during the summer personally conducted tours to the principal crypts and cemeteries of France will be organized by the proprietors of the paper.

—*East Oregonian* [Pendleton, OR], 13 August, 1910: p. 7.

The mute's professional silence was also a source of humor.

Just as the jurymen were about to be sworn, the judge interposed and said, "Make that gentleman understand that he must stand down." The officer of the Court spoke to the juryman indicated, but he did not answer, nor did he appear to understand what was wanted. After much trouble he was induced to leave the box. He had "got round" someone to tell the judge that he was "a mute." So he was—a "funeral mute."

—*Law Notes: A Monthly Magazine for Students and Practitioners*, Vol. VII., Albert Gibson et al. editors, 1888: p. 263.

In 1891 mutes were remembered with satirical faux-nostalgia:

A TEAR FOR THE VANISHED MUTE.

More losses we've had than I care to compute,
But the saddest of all is the loss of our Mute.
I shall always remember his figure austere,
Which filled me in childhood with mystical fear.
As I saw him lugubrious, silent and slow,
Keeping desolate watch at some mansion of woe,
How greasy his hat was! How seedy his clothes!
How shaggy his eyebrows! How rosy his nose!
His gloves didn't fit him, no more did his shoes,
His hands and his feet in them both he might lose.
He seemed to have borrowed some other man's legs;
The cup of mock anguish he drenched to the dregs.
And yet to my mem'ry he'll ever appear
A compound delightful of sorrow and beer.
He was paid to look wretched and can't be rebuked,

The more money he got the more wretched he looked,
His honesty, therefore, no man could dispute,
So we'll all shed a tear for the Funeral Mute.

—*Judy: The London Serio-Comic Journal.* 30 September, 1891: p. 158.

The Last Word

In 1843, mutes were paid from 18s. to 30s. Two London mutes with their covered staffs cost the equivalent of US$9.63 in 1851. And in 1844, an undertaker said that he paid an employee 5s. as a coffin bearer, but 6s. as a mute, if "he put on an extra solemn face," although the customary fee for a mute was 5s. 6d.

—*Woolmer's Exeter and Plymouth Gazette*
[Exeter, Devon, England], 30 November, 1844: p. 4.

N for Necropolis

Destination sublime

For corpses and mourners

The end of the line

When churchyards in London and its environs filled up with corpses, sometimes multiple layers deep, [See CHURCHYARDS] there was a move to create "garden" cemeteries outside of the city. These were designed to be welcoming places where families would come to stroll and picnic and visit their loved ones' graves.

This new type of burial place was called a necropolis, from the Greek phrase meaning "City of the Dead." They were large cemeteries with elaborate monuments, built outside of the crowded cities, in park-like settings with trees and winding lanes. The term eventually came to mean any planned metropolitan cemetery. It was also co-opted by the London Necropolis & National Mausoleum Company, formed in 1854, to take advantage of the garden cemetery trend, after London's overcrowded graveyards were closed to burials in 1851.

The major London cemeteries like Highgate and Kensal Green were only reachable by hearse. The London Necropolis company both established Brookwood Cemetery in Woking, Surrey (also known as Woking Necropolis) and linked it to London with a dedicated railway line: The London Necropolis Railway.

Mourners boarded the rail line at Waterloo Station, where special hearse vans were reserved for coffins. There were separate waiting rooms and train compartments for Church of England mourners and the Nonconformist or Dissenter bereaved, as well as other faiths. Fares for the melancholy journey were cheap, if not cheerful.

> The charge for taking the dead from the Waterloo station will not amount to 6d. per coffin—the fares for mourners, back and forward, being first class 6s., second class 3s 6d., and third class 2s.
>
> —*Extramural Interment and the Metropolitan Sanitary Association, Letter to The Right Hon. The Earl of Derby and Lord John Manners On the Dead Man's Question,* Sir Richard Broun[1], 1852: p. 11.

[1] One of the original architects of the London Necropolis proposal.

At the time, Brookwood Cemetery was the largest cemetery in the world.

> The largest cemetery serving the Metropolitan area is, of course, at Brookwood. Notwithstanding its distance from London, it has a gate, so to speak, in Westminster Bridge Road in the form of the Necropolis Company's private station....The waiting-rooms—one of which is allotted for the exclusive use of every party of mourners attending a private funeral—are bright and furnished in admirable taste. While there is nothing funereal about them, no gloomy black with its morbid associations, they are free from any jarring note. The same good taste is shown in other parts of the station, which contains every convenience that can possibly be desired, including a beautifully fitted mortuary chapel.
>
> At the platform stands a train—the train of the dead. On the door of the guard's van are two or three small cards bearing names, one of which, you notice, is the same as that on a similar ticket at the entrance to a waiting-room, while some of the compartments are reserved in like manner. Two mourners are already seated in readiness for the journey, silent, thoughtful, a little sad maybe. They are Chelsea pensioners, and they are taking to his rest an old comrade whom Death has claimed at last.
>
> Thus are London's dead conveyed to Woking, normally at the rate of three or four thousand yearly, though as many as fifty bodies have been sent down in a day. Sometimes a "special" is ordered for the funeral of a great man, but as a general rule all classes alike go down in the regular daily train.
>
> —*Living London*, George R. Sims, 1902: pp. 83-84.

The railway was praised for its efficiency, yet it was thought that it lacked a certain amount of funereal decorum.

> **THE LAST RIDE**
>
> There is a curious sombre little station in the Westminster Bridge road from which daily dozens of persons make their last railway journey in this world....

Throughout every day in the year the bodies are arriving at the station mortuary, until when the eleven o'clock coffin express is ready to start, there are from thirty to seventy corpses booked as passengers, for whom the railway journey, with its fields and flowers and hedges *en route* presents no attractions—passengers who are never likely to grumble at the speed of the train. But between the mortuary and the train the visitor may witness a singular spectacle. The defunct patrons of the line must be lifted from the mortuary below to the platform above. This lift is worked by hand, and the man who works it bears, through the nature of his occupation, an extraordinary similitude to Charon ferrying the dead across the Styx. The operation is a painfully slow one, but, as may be divined, nobody is in any hurry.

The guard of the train boasts of having taken down nearly 30,000 corpses in his time. In the old days the coffin train used to depart from Waterloo about midnight....

It must not be supposed that the whole train is given up to the dead, however, for a large number of mourners are invariably carried, and when the train draws up at Brookwood Cemetery there is even a refreshment room where a little full bodied cheerfulness can be imbibed and generated....

All the third-class or parish bodies are transferred to hearses drawn by three horses, capable of accommodating a matter of six or eight coffins, and the loading having been quickly done—but in unsentimental, workmanlike fashion—the biers are soon on their way to the respective graves.

From the beginning to the end of this business there is little to inspire a sense of the melancholy or funereal—not even a single sable plume; nothing to suggest the awfulness, the solemnity of the rite; certainly not the speed of the train, which might easily give points to the South-Eastern express. Truly this is a twentieth century *cortege!*

—*Cork [Ireland] Weekly News,* 29 January, 1898: p. 2.

Although the cemetery's beauty and the railway's thoughtful arrangements were widely praised in the press, the company struggled to make a profit. The numbers of burials needed to make the scheme live up to the rosy prospectus of the London Necropolis Company never quite materialized.

The London station was destroyed in a bombing raid in 1941, ending the funeral trains to Brookwood.

The Last Word

Despite the Necropolis Railway being called the "Stiff Express" or the "Corpse Carrier," the line's access to Woking golf courses made it popular with golfers, who would disguise themselves as mourners to take advantage of the cheap fares. There is no word on how they disguised their golf clubs, although the idea of the faux-mourners packing a coffin with clubs is a diverting one.

O is for Obelisk
Egyptian-themed tomb
Evokes pharaoh's pyramids
But takes up less room

How did the obelisk, a symbol of the Egyptian sun god Ra, enter the iconography of the Christian burial ground?

The obelisk is a common form of Victorian funeral monument. It is a tapering, four-sided pillar topped with a pyramid-like shape, like the Washington Monument.

These grave markers were inspired by the obelisks of Egypt, although they may, like the spires of churches, represent the soul ascending to heaven.

Obelisks became popular about the same time that "garden cemeteries" came into use, offering a spiritual, yet secular place for burial. Archaeological excavations reported in the press created interest in ancient civilizations, which led to several periods of "Egyptian Revival" style in decorative arts and architecture. The Grove Street Cemetery in New Haven, Connecticut, built on an older burial ground of 1636, chose to build an Egyptian Revival gateway in 1845 to reinforce the antiquity of the site. Highgate Cemetery in London is famous for its Egyptian Avenue. Viewed as an emblem of long-buried civilizations, obelisks symbolized timelessness and Eternity.

Obelisks may be found in white bronze (see ZINC), slate, and granite. They were also a popular motif on mourning embroideries. Americans liked to put their own particular touch on them.

> Many of our readers will recall the hieroglyphics illustrated in these columns some months ago, as being the inscription to be cut on a large monument then under construction at the Barre Works of C.E. Tayntor & Co., of New York city. The monument was completed last month and now stands in Greenwood Cemetery, Brooklyn. The obelisk is 51 feet in height and weighs approximately 50 tons, it is the second largest monolith in America. The monument was ordered by Mr. John Stemme, a retired real estate dealer who is said to have conceived the idea of having a monster monolith for his monument while sojourning in Egypt. The hieroglyphics referred to stand for the family name.
>
> —*The Monumental News*, August, 1896: p. 528.

The anonymous authors of the *Rules and Regulations of the Green-wood Cemetery*, of Brooklyn, seemed to have a certain animosity towards obelisks; they are mentioned multiple times in the book, but rarely in flattering terms.

> In most of our rural cemeteries, the popular taste, one to a servile imitation, has shown a strong predilection for pyramidic forms. The chief objection is the multiplication of one thing producing, as it must, a wearisome sameness. We have seen a ground so full of pyramids and obelisks, that one could fancy it a gigantic cabinet of minerals, being all crystals set on end....The great pyramid of Gizeh excites emotions of grandeur by its vast height and bulk. Reduce it to a model six feet high: the sublimity is gone, and there is no special beauty in the object to compensate for the loss. Those vast monolithal, acicular pyramids called obelisks, their summits piercing the skies, and their adamantine surfaces embossed with hieroglyphics, attract our gaze as marvels of patience and power. But what particular...charm have our petty and unsuccessful imitations of them, that they should usurp...so much space?
>
> These remarks, it is scarcely necessary to add, urge not the exclusion of this class of monuments, but only a more sparing and sensible use of them....
>
> Those whose hearts are set on pyramids and obelisks, will of course gratify that taste. While so doing, it may be well to remember, that...these seemingly monotonous structures differ very considerably,—often betraying, by their clumsiness, the bungling ignorance of those who designed them....
>
> —*Rules and Regulations of the Green-wood Cemetery.*
> New York, N.Y., 1849: pp. 17, 53-54.

The Last Word

The tallest obelisk tombstone in the United States is a 150-foot granite obelisk in Philadelphia's Woodlands Cemetery, marking the grave of Dr. Thomas Wiltberger Evans, dentist to the crowned heads of Europe, who died in 1897.

P is post-mortem—
The last portrait made
Securing the shadow
Ere loved likeness fade

Post-mortem photography is perhaps the most widely-known—and most widely misunderstood—Victorian mourning custom. While portraits of loved ones on their deathbeds had been painted and sculpted for centuries, the new technology of photography guaranteed that the bereaved could "secure the shadow, ere the substance fade."

> How sublime the thought that man, by a simple process, can constrain the light of heaven to catch and fix the fleeting shadow of life, even as it lingers upon the pallid features of death.
>
> Hail glorious light that thus can timely save
> The beauty of our loved ones from the grave!
>
> —*The Photographic and Fine Art Journal*, Vol. 8. July, 1858: p. 224.

The earliest examples are daguerreotypes and ambrotypes, images captured on silvered metal or glass plates respectively. These fragile images were kept in hinged cases of leather, metal or gutta percha. Post-mortem photographs also might be framed with a coffin plate, waxed funeral flowers or hairwork wreaths.

Most subjects were portrayed reclining, as if asleep, some in their coffins, some on a chaise lounge or sofa. Infants were sometimes laid in a crib or baby carriage. This cautious photographer shares one of his secrets for giving the illusion of sleep.

> Having examined the certificate of death, to guard myself from any such disasters as catching the measles or whooping cough, or transferring the same undesirable maladies to my customers, I proceed to the chamber where the shadow of death hath cast its awful gloom....Here, in the hallowed and mysterious presence of the sweet little innocent, it is indeed difficult to follow mercenary pursuits....Having arranged the blankets in such a manner as would form a little bed, I altered the position of the Venetian blinds, so as to throw a decided but soft shade on to the face....With regard to position, I take the greatest care not to show the nostrils. I have in this way always managed to produce pictures which were more sleep than deathlike.
>
> —*The Photographic News,* 8 April, 1887: p. 221.

A few post-mortem subjects are posed in chairs. It is a popular myth that metal posing stands, used to hold the head still for a long photographic exposure, were used to stand corpses up for their portraits. It is claimed that if you can see the base of a posing stand behind a subject, it means that the person is actually dead. This is not true—posing stands are not sturdy enough to hold up the dead-weight of a corpse. There are descriptions from coroners and law-enforcement officers of the stout tables, chairs, and straps that were used to pose a corpse upright for forensic identification. In the extensive professional photographic literature, there is absolutely no mention of propping up bodies with posing stands for commercial post mortems.

Photographers were also sometimes called upon to photograph the dying—producing a pre-mortem photograph. It was a trying experience and some examples make grim viewing.

The practice of photographing the dead was regarded with distaste by some professional photographers.

> [Post-mortem photography] is the craze that astonishes me. It shows as deep a morbid hankering, in my estimation, as those who travel miles to look at a house where a murder has been committed, and go away happy if they can secure a bit of plaster or a chip of brick off the ill-fated house. How the relatives can bear to look upon these photographs I cannot understand, unless they have a peculiar love for the horrible. For my part I cannot see the necessity of photographing the dead at all. If the departed were truly beloved, nothing that may happen in this world can ever efface the dear features from the mind's eye; it needs not a cold, crude photograph representing the last dreary stage of humanity to recall those lineaments. Indeed, I should imagine it would in time lead to the forgetting of the pleasant smile or the lightsome laugh, and supply, in place, a ghoul-like resemblance of anything but a pleasant nature. Then look what cold blankets these photographs prove! If a pleasant party is assembled and the family album produced, just observe how the fun collapses when one of those

buried subjects turns up! Do what you like, the rest of the evening has a shadow on it.

—*The Photographic News*, 7 July, 1882: pp. 394-395.

Post-mortem photographs were also taken of the unidentified dead at morgues around the world in the hopes that eventually someone would recognize them.

> There is a man in New York who makes a business of photographing corpses. He takes a picture of the face of every dead person who turns up at the morgue in that city. The likenesses are mounted on cards and kept in a little cabinet at the morgue office. In each case the photograph is made without arranging the hair or in any other way modifying the appearance of the defunct, inasmuch as to do so might interfere with the recognition of the latter by friends. Sometimes, after years have passed, relatives of these unfortunate individuals find out their fate by seeing their features on the cards. Suicides are often neatly shaved and dressed, as if they had prepared themselves particularly to have their pictures taken. The likenesses in the cabinet run all the way back to 1868.
>
> —*The Courier-Journal* [Louisville, KY], 22 June, 1896: p. 3.

A great many post-mortem photographs were of children because of high rates of infant mortality. It was a way to secure a likeness of a beloved child if they had never before had a photograph taken. It was also seen as a comfort to the bereaved parents.

> Usually it is a child the photographer is called upon to photograph, the reason being that most adults have at some period of their life been portrayed, and an enlargement from that portrait is generally preferred to a *post-mortem* picture. But children are often cut off before they have ever been photographed, and the desire to have something to remember them by, and to recall their once-familiar features, must be taken as the excuse for the existence of this class of work at all.
>
> —*The British Journal of Photography*, 3 August, 1883: pp. 449-50.

I've been engaged in taking pictures of the dead for twenty years or more, was the remark of a photographer of Philadelphia, as he arranged his camera to photograph the first corpse ever brought to a Philadelphia gallery for that purpose. A little coffin or casket was under the sky-light in a slanting position, supported by two chairs, and in it was the body of a fair-haired child, whose peaceful, smiling expression, despite the ghastly pallor of death, make it appear to be in tranquil sleep. The head lay in a perfect bed of flowers, and the waxen hands clasped held a spray of mignonette and two delicate tea rosebuds. The sun, shaded as it was by curtains, threw a bright glare over one side of the little dead face, leaving the other half in shadow....It only took a moment, and there was really nothing awful about it. The mother, poor soul, will have something to look at and cry over now.

—*Cincinnati [OH] Enquirer,* 1 April, 1882: p. 12.

The Last Word

Although today the phrase "memento mori" is often used to describe post-mortem photographs, an extensive search of 19th- and early 20th-century photographic journals, as well as references to post-mortem photography in newspapers and magazines, finds absolutely no evidence to indicate that this term was ever used by Victorians or Edwardians to describe those cherished final images.

Q for Queen Victoria
England's mourner in chief
Wrapped in her crape
And her obsessive grief

Rudyard Kipling dubbed her "The Widow of Windsor," but Queen Victoria might well have been called The Empress of Grief. She was surrounded by death from an early age. Her father, Prince Edward, Duke of Kent and Strathearn, died when she was only 8 months old. A week later, her grandfather, George III died. None of her uncles had legitimate heirs, so Victoria became queen when William IV died in 1837.

Perhaps the Queen's losses were no more numerous than those of an average British family, but her bereavements were more public and her grief more protracted. Although estranged from her mother, the Duchess of Kent, Victoria was heart-broken when her mother died in March, 1861. In December, 1861, Victoria suffered the greatest loss of all, the death of her beloved husband, Prince Albert, who was only 42. The death of Prince Albert plunged the Queen into a lengthy and obsessive period of mourning. She was criticized for selfishly retreating from public duty to indulge her grief. Victoria was indignant over these criticisms, stating that no one could understand what she suffered. There were rumors that she had gone mad or that she was about to abdicate, and there were fears that the monarchy would be overthrown.

Multiple friends and royal relatives predeceased the Queen: her uncle, Leopold I, King of the Belgians; her half-sister, Princess Feodora of Leiningen; her second daughter, Alice, who died of diphtheria on the anniversary of Prince Albert's death; her son Alfred, of throat cancer; her youngest son, Leopold, a hemophiliac, of bleeding after a fall; grandson Prince Albert Victor, known to the family as "Eddy," heir to the throne, of influenza; and John Brown, her beloved Highland servant. Death seemed to follow the Queen and she coped by immersing herself in the minutiae of mourning. But it is one thing to be resigned; it is another to seem to revel in death and its accoutrements.

The American press was unsympathetic about what they called the Queen's morbid passion for death.

> Royalty with the great majority [of the English] is so closely associated with regal pomp and show, that they have no patience with

> a mourning court or a Queen who continuously wears the habiliments of a widow's woe.
>
> —*The Millinery Trade Review*, March, 1876: p. 30.

> Queen Victoria is never so happy as when sitting by a death bed.
>
> —*Daily Illinois State Register* [Springfield, IL], 24 October, 1889: p. 3.

> To an earnest believer in the Christian religion, one who regards the body as merely the casket of the departed soul, it seems almost wicked, the attention paid here to this lifeless casket. Hours are spent in graveyards, and doubtless fatal colds contracted on the anniversaries of the mournful day of burial. People indulge in grief with a morbid extravagance that is quite unaccountable to the philosophic mind. They seem to find a luxury in woe. And who can wonder after all when the example is constantly set them by the first lady in the land, Her Majesty the Queen, who spends hours at the mausoleum at Frognal [*sic*] on the anniversary deathdays of those whom she loved in life, placing fresh wreaths on the tombs, holding dirgelike religious services, weeping and making herself and her family generally miserable....
>
> Naturally, the Queen's example is emulated by the wife of the mechanic, who periodically and solemnly wends her way to the grave of her dead, laden with flowers, both natural and, likelier still, cheap artificial ones, covered over with glass globes, than which there can be nothing more ghastly.
>
> —*Boston [MA] Herald,* 15 July, 1894: p. 25.

While *The Delineator* of October, 1895 stated that "the Royal Widow of England has fixed the fashions for all the widows of her realm and of America," the Queen did not invent Victorian mourning. Elaborate rituals for court mourning had been part of royal obsequies for centuries and the French had an intricate system of civil *pompes funèbres*, which spelled out every detail of different classes of funeral. However, Queen Victoria set the tone for English and American mourning—we might call her the "top influencer" of mourning. People of all social classes aspired to copy royal mourning rituals as much as they could afford, to show a fitting respect for their own dead. And, while she might be criticized for choosing to wear mourning for Prince Albert for the rest of her life, the Queen still would have spent many of her years in black for family members, who were scattered across Europe.

> The Q. said to Lady C. Harrington the other day, that she had been nine months in mourning each year for the last three or four, and had lost ten uncles and aunts since her marriage; and Lady Caroline said that if she had not been afraid it would hardly have been respectful, she felt much inclined to ask, "And pray, Ma'am, how many more have you to lose?"
>
> —*Twenty Years at Court, 1842-1862 from the Correspondence of the Hon. Eleanor Stanley, Maid of Honour to Her late Majesty Queen Victoria 1842-1862.* Mrs Steuart Erskine, editor. 1916: p. 205.

> The advocates of modern funeral reform might complain that Her Majesty was too punctilious in her outward signs of mourning; but, as she once playfully said to Lord Melbourne in her young days, "What is the use of being a queen if you cannot do as you like?" It is said that she refused to sign a Commission because the paper was not bordered with black; and we know that for at least eight years after the Prince Consort's death the royal servants wore a band of crape upon the left arm, while in her own attire Her Majesty has never, throughout the succeeding years of her widowhood, worn any but mourning colours....At her command the late Prince's apartments at Windsor, Osborne, and Balmoral were closed, and remain to-day exactly as they were at his death....
>
> Not only were the Prince's rooms preserved in the state in which he left them—a custom which the Queen follows with all her nearest departed relatives—but her own boudoir at Windsor Castle is kept in the same state to-day as it was when the Prince Consort died. On the door is inscribed, "Every article in this room my lamented husband selected for me in the twenty-fourth year of my reign." In this room the Queen's bridal wreath and the first

> bouquet which the Prince presented to her lie withered in a glass case.
>
> —*The Personal Life of Queen Victoria.*
> Sarah A. Southall Tooley. 1897: pp. 204-206.

The Queen had decided opinions about how others should mourn. She wrote this to her daughter, Victoria, the Princess Royal, at the German court.

> I think it quite wrong that the nursery are not in mourning, at any rate I should make them wear grey or white or drab—and baby wear white and lilac, but not colours. That I think shocking. Well of course with your German relations you must I suppose do what is custom—but you must promise me that if I should die your child or children and those around you should mourn; this really must be, for I have such strong feeling on this subject, which certainly is, to say the least, more reasonable than leaving the rooms of dear relatives left for years as mausoleums particularly in the midst of other people's rooms.
>
> —*Dearest Child: Letters between Queen Victoria and the Princess Royal, Previously Unpublished.*
> Roger Fulford, editor. 1964: pp. 199-200.

The Queen was referring to the room in the Royal Palace of Berlin in which Frederick William III had died, which was preserved by his sons as "the death room." Singularly ironic, considering how she kept Prince Albert's room at Windsor as a shrine.

The Queen was a keen advocate of mourning crape. Most etiquette books disapproved of children being put into deep mourning—especially very young children. But the Queen was adamant that her children should wear crape. In 1860 she rhapsodized over her youngest daughter, Princess Beatrice, then aged three, wearing mourning for her half-sister's husband, Ernst I, Prince of Hohenlohe-Langenburg, writing, "Darling Beatrice looks lovely in her black silk and crepe [*sic*] dress."

In photographs from this period, Darling Beatrice looks singularly dissatisfied, especially in photographs of her with the Queen, who is smothering her in a crape-trimmed embrace.

Although it is doubtful that the Queen was aware of it, she and her eldest daughter, the Dowager Empress Frederick of Germany, appeared in advertisements for Grout & Co., wearing deepest mourning and captioned, "Portraits of the Queen of England and Empress of Germany wearing Grout's crapes." The advertisement further asserted:

> "By pure merit....Grout's Crapes
> Have been selected and are being worn by the
> Royal Families of England and Germany."
>
> —*Textile America, Organ of the Textile Division of Commerce.* 7 August, 1897: p. 5.

The Queen's attention to the details of mourning made life difficult for her attendants. In 1860 one of her Maids of Honour, the Hon. Eleanor Stanley described to her mother some of the uncertainties and apparently arbitrary decisions about the requirements of mourning.

> This is the birthday of Princess of Leiningen, and we were told that we might, if we *liked*, make our mourning a little slighter in consequence; this seemed such a very confused message that I have just been asking Miss Skerrett about it, and she said she would find out, but that the Queen was in black herself this morning, and she was pretty sure H.M. meant to wear black this evening again. We have just got the order, which is, to wear white gloves, white or lilac flowers, coloured jewellery, and black silk or lace. Really these niceties are too plaguy! [*sic*] To-morrow we go into white or grey—for Princess Royal's birthday—and the next day plunge back into the depths of sorrow....
>
> —*Twenty Years at Court, 1842-1862 from the Correspondence of the Hon. Eleanor Stanley, Maid of Honour to Her late Majesty Queen Victoria 1842-1862*. Mrs Steuart Erskine, editor. 1916: pp. 376-377.

1900 was indeed an *annus horribilis* for the Queen. Her second son, Alfred, died 30 July 1900, of throat cancer. Prince Christian Victor of Schleswig-Holstein, the Queen's grandson by her daughter Helena, died 29 October 1900 of typhoid fever in South Africa. A close friend of the Queen, The Dowager Lady Churchill, Senior Lady of the Bedchamber, was found dead in her bed at Osborne House 24 December 1900. Queen Victoria mourned in her diary: "It is a horrible year, nothing but sadness & horrors of one kind & another." The Queen herself was dead within the month, dying on 22 January 1901, a day before the anniversary of her father's death.

The Last Word

The Queen who had spent most of her life in black, requested a white funeral, with white ponies to pull her white-draped coffin on a gun carriage. She wanted no embalming, no lying in state, no crape draperies. She was buried in a white dress and her wedding veil; the coffin was covered with a white pall.

At the chapel of St George, Windsor:

> The profusion of flowers displayed outside the chapel ceased within. On the chancel only a few lilies and the most delicate green ferns were used for the altar decorations.
>
> There was no crape anywhere.
>
> —*Queen Victoria: Her Grand Life and Glorious Reign.* John Coulter and John A. Cooper. 1901: p. 236.

R for Resurrection Men

The dread churchyard crooks

They dig up fresh corpses

With spade, sack, and hooks

If there was one thing the Victorians feared more than burial alive, it was the resurrectionists, or body snatchers, also known as "sack-'em-up men." These enterprising entrepreneurs dug up fresh corpses to sell to medical schools, which used the cadavers to teach anatomy. Medical schools were officially restricted to using the bodies of the indigent, the unclaimed, or the executed for this purpose, but there were never enough corpses available. This created a lively trade in stolen bodies. Corpses might be shipped to medical schools in barrels labeled as pork or fish, which would account for any unpleasant smells.

There was a good deal of ghoulish fascination with the lurid details of grave robbing. This description comes from an interview with Charles Keeton, a resurrection man of Cincinnati, Ohio.

> "When we'd come through to the part where the graves were close together, and we knew it was the poor lot where the people without any friends are buried, then we'd dig down to the coffin, break it open and put a rope around the neck and pull the body out. I don't do that way now, though, for it is just as easy to throw all the dirt out. Then, after throwing it out, I generally get down and open the coffin, and take the body by the waist and lift it out to my partner. He takes it, and gen'ly runs a knife down the back and rips the clothes off, and lets 'em drop down. Then we slip the head into a sack, press the knees up against the chest, and slip the body in and tie the sack. That's all there is of it."
>
> "How do you enjoy the work?"
>
> "Well, it wasn't very pleasant at first, of course; but any one gets used to it. It is for the good of science, and I think it is just as right and honourable as for the man who does the dissection."
>
> —*Titusville [PA] Herald*, 11 June, 1878: p. 1.

It was vital to strip the corpse. While corpses were not considered anyone's property and thus couldn't be stolen, it was a felony to steal a shroud, a coffin, or other grave goods.

Cincinnati, Ohio also boasted a lady resurrectionist whose long and profitable career involved a bewildering assortment of husbands, paramours, and fake names. Calling her Mrs. Susie Dyer, the local paper printed a lengthy story in which she unabashedly described her methods for compactly folding a corpse.

> A jump on the body to break its back-bone would make it susceptible to doubling up, when it would be rammed into a sack and carried off to a vehicle near by.
>
> —*Cincinnati [OH] Enquirer*, 2 October, 1885: p. 8.

This passage describes the hook used to drag the body from the grave. Planted under the chin, it ensured that no organs worth studying would be damaged.

> [B]y the feeble light of their lantern, they moved on among the tombstones till they reached the designated grave. Plying spade and mattock vigorously, they paused not till the loose earth had been removed at the head of the grave and that part of the coffin where the head of the corpse reposed was exposed to view. The lid was smashed in with a blow of a crowbar and the ghastly features of the dead were revealed. But there was no time to contemplate the awful spectacle. A rope armed with an iron hook was let down into the grave. The hook catching under the lower jaw of the corpse, afforded a firm hold, and with a strong pull the stiff and lifeless mass, enveloped in its shroud, was dragged from its resting-place. Hurriedly the body was borne to the carriage, which was driven off rapidly to the dissecting-room, while the two hired men remained behind to refill the grave and efface the traces of the night's work.
>
> —*Frank Leslie's Weekly*, 18 April, 1868: p. 71.

Although the Anatomy Act of 1832 gave anatomy schools in the United Kingdom legal access to unclaimed corpses from prisons, hospitals, and workhouses, there were never enough cadavers, so the Act did little to stop the resurrection men. Increasing demand led to shocking cases of people being murdered and their bodies sold, no questions asked, to the medical schools. There were also undertakers who buried empty coffins, turning the contents over to the doctors for cash, while collecting fees from county or parish authorities for the burial. In one case a sexton left corpses in their coffins sitting outside. In the morning the corpses would be gone and he'd bury the coffins. He said, with a shrug, that he was paid to bury a coffin, not necessarily a coffin with a corpse.

One of the most notorious body snatchers in the United States was William Cunningham, popularly called "Old Man Dead," the "Prince of Ghouls," or "Old Cunny." Born in Ireland, he was a big, muscular man with a taste for whiskey and a talent for outwitting the law when stealing corpses to sell to the Medical College of Ohio in Cincinnati. It was said that he and his fellow ghouls had been known to resurrect as many as 100 bodies per season.

When he died in 1871, no funeral was held because the old rogue had sold his own body to the Medical College of Ohio for $50, years before. Some stories say he sold himself to multiple medical schools as one final joke. His widow got another $5.00 out of the College for the corpse. After his cadaver was cut up and the bones cleaned, Old Cunny's skeleton was wired and placed in a glass case in the museum of the College, posed, hat on skull, sitting on a tombstone with a pipe in his jaws and a spade in one bony hand.

In the United States, a sensational case in Ohio in 1878 led to new legislation about corpses for medical schools being enacted on a state-by-state basis.

Body Snatching in America.

> Great excitement prevails in Ohio, caused by the prevalence of body-snatching. John Scott Harrison, formerly member of Congress from Ohio, and son of President Harrison, of the United States, died suddenly near Northbend, [*sic*] in Ohio, on Sunday, being interred there on Wednesday, in the Presbyterian cemetery. Just previously a corpse had been stolen from that cemetery, which caused extraordinary precautions to be taken in walling up Harrison's grave, covering it with heavy stones, and placing guards. Soon after the funeral Mr. Harrison's son, with others, visited Cincinnati, searching for the corpse previously stolen.

> While searching in the Ohio Medical College at Cincinnati they unexpectedly discovered Mr. Harrison's corpse suspended in a vault by a rope round the neck, the jugular vein being cut, but the body not having yet been otherwise mutilated. Much excitement followed, which has been increased by reports from Northbend that, the guards proving faithless, the grave had been despoiled. Several arrests have been made for complicity in the crime.
>
> —*Birmingham [West Midlands, England] Daily Post*, 3 June, 1878: p. 5.

Many methods were used to stop the theft of corpses: they were kept in a crypt or under a mortsafe (an iron box or cage) until too decomposed to sell. Armed watchmen roamed the cemeteries or families spent several nights in a watch tower overlooking the burying ground. Mortsafes and watchmen did not stop determined resurrectionists; deadlier measures were adopted. Devices were invented that shot or exploded when a coffin was forced open.

> Some bodies having been stolen from the church-yard of a remote parish in Northumberland, the owner of the estate, to prevent such depredations in future, has directed the graves to be made rather shorter than the coffin, and to be excavated at the bottom, so as to admit the head under the solid ground. It is then impossible to raise it by the feet, and the ground must be cut away above the head—a work of more time than could always be commanded for the operation. In addition, a mixture of percussion powder and gunpowder, placed on a wire in the inside of the coffin, to explode on its being opened, has been resorted to. This will retain its explosive power for a month, in which time the corpse will generally be unfit for dissection.
>
> —*The Bath [Avon, England] Chronicle*, 19 February, 1824: p. 3.

In 1878, an American artist named Philip K. Clover patented the formidably-named "Coffin-Torpedo."

> In consequence of the increasing number of grave-yard desecrations, the genius of the inventor has been incited to devise means for their defeat. Among the most recent patents is one for a coffin torpedo, which consists of a canister containing powder, balls and a firing trigger, so arranged that, on placing the torpedo within the coffin, and finally closing the lid, should any attempt be made to open the coffin the torpedo will be instantly exploded, a noise like thunder ensue, and deadly balls will fly in all directions.
>
> *Scientific American*, 30 November, 1878: p. 337.

It is impossible to know how often these devices were deployed, but here is an incident from 1881.

A GRAVE STORY.
A Torpedo Placed as a Sentinel.

> Mount Vernon, O, January 19. On Monday night last three men attempted a grave robbery near Gann, in this county, and when nearing the bottom of the grave which they were excavating, they struck a torpedo that had been placed on top of the coffin for protection, instantly killing a man named Dipper and breaking a leg of one whose name has not been ascertained. The third party, who was keeping watch, succeeded in getting his companions into a sleigh, taking flight, and evading arrest.
>
> —*The Philadelphia [PA] Inquirer,* 20 January, 1881: p. 8.

Less lethal methods included fastening the corpse into the coffin with an iron hoop round the neck and holding the coffin in a crypt until the body was too decomposed to be used for dissection. In the end, it may have been a plain pine box that stymied the resurrectionists.

> "The body snatching business ceased to be profitable [said one cemetery superintendent] when we began to use the pine box to inclose [*sic*] the coffin or casket. Before the introduction of this outer box it was comparatively easy for the grave robber to make a narrow excavation at the head of the grave, lift the wooden lid over the glass through which the face of the corpse is seen, smash

> the glass, insert a body hook under the chin and jerk the body out of the grave. But now the whole grave must be excavated and the lid of the pine box unscrewed before the coffin is accessible. This takes so much time and so increases the chances of discovery that few care to engage in the business for the money there is in it."
>
> —*Delphos [OH] Daily Herald*, 31 December, 1897, p. 3.

Like other grisly topics relating to Victorian death and mourning, body snatching also became a subject of dark humor.

> [A] resurrectionist...having purloined a body from a burial-ground, took it to Dr.__. When he had received his pay, and was just about to depart, the Doctor perceived the body move, and exclaimed, "Why, you scoundrel, it's alive!"
>
> "Is it," said the man; "well, then, kill it when you want it."
>
> —*The Observer* [London, England], 11 January, 1829: p. 4.

The Last Word

Although the most famous so-called body snatchers were William Burke and William Hare of Edinburgh, Scotland, they were not actually resurrection men, but common murderers.

William Hare kept a lodging house and when an old tenant died owing back rent, Burke suggested selling the body to a local anatomist. Finding it easy money, the duo murdered some sixteen local people to sell to anatomist Dr. Robert Knox, giving us the term "to burke," for homicidal suffocation, and inspiring the rhyme:

> Up the close and doon the stair,
> But and ben' wi' Burke and Hare.
> Burke's the butcher, Hare's the thief,
> Knox the boy that buys the beef.

Burke was hanged and his skin used to bind the testimony from his trial. Hare turned king's evidence and was released. His fate afterwards is unknown.

S is for Shroud
In fashionable style
Beribboned and laced—
Grim Death to beguile

The word "shroud" originally meant a winding sheet—a large piece of cloth wound around the body and sometimes tied at head and foot like a Christmas cracker. A shroud might also be a garment, something like a nightgown, made with an opening up the back for ease of dressing the deceased. A shroud could also be a burial suit modelled on fashionable clothing—finished on the front, but backless.

> To see them in their coffins you would think they were completely dressed, but really all their finery is on top. Even the men's solid looking black coats and smooth shirt fronts can go on and off without removing the corpse.
>
> —*Huron Daily Huronite* [Huron, SD], 16 January, 1890: p. 3.

As a matter of local custom, the Victorian poor and the rural dead were often buried simply in a shroud, without a coffin. While the definition of a "decent" burial included a coffin and a shroud, the shroud was the essential part of burial. Although the Biblical passage stated "Naked I came from my mother's womb, and naked shall I return," it was thought scandalous, even sacrilegious, to bury a corpse unshrouded.

From the early- to the mid-1800s, shrouds were made by friends or family of the deceased. In addition, in response to the possibility of death in childbirth, brides might make a shroud to include in their trousseau. In some communities, practical persons made shrouds just in case, to be kept under the bed or in the "death drawer," a personalized cache of burial clothing.

> The burial of Mrs. Abraham Lesher at Kleinfeltersville, the other day, with her sixty-five-year-old black silk wedding-gown for a shroud brings to notice a queer East Pennsylvania custom which prevails among German farmers. Nearly all the people, old and young, have their shrouds and grave-clothes all ready when death comes....Indeed, it is a common thing to find a special bureau-drawer set apart for the grave-clothes. One custom is to keep every vestige of the wedding outfit for the interment apparel. Gown and undergarments are in many cases worn but once by the bride, and

> then laid away to wait for her death....Where wedding-gowns are not saved, the women folks make their own shrouds, cutting them out, sewing and trimming them....
>
> Not only do the elderly women provide a grave or death drawer, but young wives and young girls do the same thing. They begin early in life to accumulate their death trousseau....On rainy Sunday afternoons many a housewife on the Pennsylvania German farms spends an hour or so looking through her death drawer to see that nothing has been left unprovided for. If she attends a funeral and sees something new in the shape of a collar, piece of lace, handkerchief, eiderdown blanket, embroidery or anything else that may strike her fancy, she'll buy it on her first visit to town and put it in her death drawer.
>
> —*The Sun* [New York, NY], 18 February, 1900: p. 27.

Beginning in the 1870s, shrouds came to be called by the euphemistic term "burial robes." These reflected Gilded Age fashions. Women's burial robes, with their embellishments of lace and embroidery, were lovingly described by journalists in the same language used by fashion writers for wedding gowns or tea gowns.

> There is many a shroud made in this city that would pass muster as a tea gown straight from Paris. The finest and loveliest of materials from softest cashmere to richest silk, filmy laces, jaunty ribbons, chiffon and mousseline de soie enter into the composition of the up-to-date shroud....The shrouds, as shrouds, are a sheer disappointment. They are so utterly unshroud-like....
>
> —*Buffalo [NY] Morning Express and Illustrated Buffalo Express*, 18 October, 1897: p. 6.

Towards the end of the nineteenth century, the use of the deceased person's own clothing became more widespread. This undertaker had an explanation for the trend:

> A prominent undertaker, who has what is known in the business as a "tony trade," said: "I don't suppose I have used more than half

> a dozen shrouds a year. With my class of trade the custom is dying out. The people I bury are nearly all cared for in their sickness by professional nurses....Well, the professional nurses in the past five years have got to preparing the dead for burial and they can dress a corpse just as well as they can a live person. My customers prefer to have their relatives buried in either the clothes they wore in life or a similar suit. A great many people I bury now are buried in their dress suit that they have worn at weddings, receptions, balls or banquets. It takes two persons to dress a body, but it is done easily nowadays. Five or six years ago it was looked upon as almost an impossibility, and up to that time nearly every body was buried in shrouds. For my part, I like to see a person prepared for the grave to look as natural as they did in life, and they certainly don't look like themselves if they are attired in a shroud."
>
> —*Liberty [TX] Vindicator,* 24 August, 1888: p. 4.

From about the mid-nineteenth century onward, the making of shrouds became part of the commercial fashion industry; they were produced in factories. Shroud-making paid unusually well to compensate for such "macabre" work and the working hours were usually shorter than those in a regular dressmaking establishment.

> The girls themselves with one accord agree that it is vastly better [working in a shroud factory] than working in dress-making shops for as one who has had experience in each line succinctly remarked:
>
> "It's a sight easier working for the dead than the living, because you see there's no kicking about the fit."
>
> —*Buffalo [NY] Morning Express and Illustrated Buffalo Express,* 18 October, 1897: p. 6.

After the First World War, commercially-made shrouds for women were called "slumber robes." These negligee-like garments were often modelled on live models at funeral trade shows and in trade catalogues.

BLONDES NEEDED TO IMITATE DEAD
Embalmers to Show Shroud Styles Fitted to Models.

Oakland, Cal., Aug. 25. Three languid blondes—the blonder and more languid the better—are wanted immediately at the annual convention of the California Undertakers' and Embalmers' Association in session here.

They are needed to fill caskets at the coffin display, but they must be alive. Albeit it is demanded that they have the necessary ability to imitate a corpse.

"Styles in shrouds, you know," said the secretary of the association, "change rapidly—particularly feminine shrouds. We feel that in order to show the latest in such perquisites to the funeral we must have living models."

The girls will be dressed in the latest of burial robes and their duty will be to lie quietly in caskets so the merry embalmers may view the latest creations....

—*Pittsburgh [PA] Daily Post,* 26 August, 1920: p. 1.

The Last Word

In the late nineteenth and early twentieth century, the word "shroud" was journalistic shorthand for any burial garment, often used in headlines like "Bride's dress becomes her shroud."

T for tear bottle
Of pretty gilt glass
They held smelling salts
And not tears, alas

One of the myths of Victorian mourning is that mourners caught their tears in tiny bottles. It is a touching picture: sobbing, black-clad mourners holding little glass vials to their eyes to catch their streaming tears. The vials could be sealed and left at the gravesite or taken home as a reminder of loss. By the time the trapped tears evaporated, perhaps the bereaved one's eyes would be dry, symbolizing an end to mourning and the renewal of hope.

Sadly, there is no documentation to suggest that this was an actual custom. The pretty antique bottles described today as tear bottles actually held perfumes or smelling salts.

The Victorian public would have been familiar with the idea of catching tears in bottles from the Biblical verse, Psalm 56: 8: "Thou tellest my wanderings: put thou my tears into thy bottle...." In addition, small glass and clay bottles found in ancient graves inspired 19th-century archaeologists and scholars to describe mourners shedding tears into these vials. The artifacts were dubbed "lacrymatories" from the Greek word for "tears," although modern science tells us that the bottles held oils, cosmetics, and medicines.

Newspapers also wrote of people in far-off lands catching tears in bottles and the term "tear bottle" was used to describe someone displaying excessive emotion. The phrase is often the equivalent of "get out your handkerchiefs!" and evokes in a jocular way fake sorrow or exaggerated grief.

But a survey of 19th-century fiction and non-fiction sources reveals no trace of the actual use of tear bottles. Since mourning fads and fashions were so well covered by the popular press, if tear bottles were used by mourners, we would expect to see them mentioned or advertised. While absence of evidence is not necessarily evidence of absence, in this case the sources—or lack of them—suggest that it is time to put the stopper into the tear-bottle myth.

Here are four items from the 19th-century press discussing tear bottles. The first two refer to an ancient, long-forgotten custom and not a mourning curiosity of a decade or two before. The third describes the appearance of vinaigrette/smelling salts bottles, which are often claimed to be "tear bottles." The last is a satire about how useful the [non-existent] bottles will be.

> I must now direct your attention to a remarkable classical curiosity, namely the "Tear Bottle." No one quite knows what these bottles were, neither is the origin known of the strange title to an Italian wine called Lachrymae Christi. This name has but correspondential value, but the tear-bottles have reference to some strange ceremonies long ago lost and forgotten.
>
> —*The Journal of the Alchemical Society*, London, November, 1913: pp. 26-7.

> I came across recently exquisite, narrow-necked, full-bodied, cut glass "tear bottles." Surely they are novelties, one would say. Not a bit of it. The idea is not less than two thousand years old. The tear bottles are fashioned after the pattern of the "lachrymae," as they were called, many of which have been found comparatively recently in the ruins of Pompeii and Herculaneum and among the tombs of the Greeks and Romans. They are supposed to have contained the tears of the mourners, and as these little bottles have been found plentifully among the Egyptian sarcophagi, it may have given rise to the well-known expression "Crocodile tears," used to denote affected woe. In these more modern days the imitation tear bottles of cut glass and porcelain which stand on the dressing tables of our belles hold something more reviving than tear drops, which helps to assuage the wrath of an angry wife or cheer the spirits of a disappointed beauty. One of these tiny bottles had around the neck in gold letters the legend: "Take a smile," the very antithesis of its former use, when the legend might appropriately have been: "Drop a tear."
>
> —*Lancaster [PA] Intelligencer,* 9 January, 1892: p. 3.

> **Revival of the Tear Bottle.**
>
> Among quaint old shapes in porcelain that are being revived are the classic "tear bottles," a narrow-necked, full-bodied shape, round at the bottom, recalling the primitive days of the human race when

> such luxuries as tables were unknown and the bottle, the chief domestic utensil, was stuck in the sand to keep it upright. The tear bottle is often found in Roman and old Greek tombs. In it were supposed to be stored the tears shed for the departed ones. Quaint bottles of porcelain in this shape are mounted in ornamental frames of wrought iron....All varieties of exquisite shapes in porcelain and Baccarat glass are mounted in wrought iron frames.
>
> —*Philadelphia [PA] Inquirer,* 16 July, 1891: p. 6.

This last quote is an excerpt from an article headed "Bottled Tears," which began by describing a craze for painting household accessories. It goes on:

> But the very latest, up to the hour of going to press is painted "tear bottles." For centuries there has been absolutely nothing to catch tears in, when a girl desired to sit down and have a good cry. How on earth this has come to be overlooked is not simply astonishing; it is astounding. Hitherto expensive handkerchiefs have been drenched, and their value nearly destroyed, on account of the sorrowing person being obliged to run to the door every few minutes and wring them out. If the person happened to be a copious weeper and her sadness of a great and overshadowing nature, like the loss of a thirteen ounce poodle, not only would the handkerchief be ruined, but all evidence of the feelings of the afflicted one over the calamity would be obliterated—wrung out in the gutter and carried away into the sewers. It is proposed now to retain these blessed mementoes in bottles, for future reference, and it is certainly a beautiful sentiment....The decanters will be labeled appropriately, "On the death of poor Carlo," "On seeing the hateful Maliflores in the loveliest of bonnets," etc. These tender tokens of past sorrows will be useful as well as sentimental, and in case the sincerity of the lady's grief is ever called in question, on the occasion of the death of her poodle or her husband, she can

set out the bottle containing the tears shed at the time, and silence the venomous tongue of slander. *Peck's Sun.*

—*Alabama Beacon* [Greensboro, AL], 16 February, 1883: p. 3.

While the headline certainly sounds authoritative, it is patently obvious from this and from the rest of the piece that the passage is meant as satire. The source also gives it away. *Peck's Sun* was run by well-known humorist George W. Peck, and was sometimes called "the funniest paper in America."

The Last Word

Author Candice Hearn makes a compelling case that the so-called tear bottles, so often offered for sale, are actually a type of scent bottle called "throwaways," "attar bottles," "Oxford lavenders," or "teardrops," due to the presence of a tiny tear-shaped cavity where the scent is found. It may be that the historic "teardrop" name led to confusion about their real use and the creation of the modern legend that these are bottles to hold tears.

U for Undertaker
The dismallest trade
He starts with a coffin
And ends with a spade

The undertaker—the term was used for any person who "undertakes" a task—began as a furniture maker or carpenter who made coffins. The job description gradually expanded to the entire management of a funeral. Ideally, the undertaker offered one-stop shopping for essential mourning products and services, supplying coffin, shroud, burial plot, hearse, carriages and such things as gloves, scarves, weepers, and door crapes. Later, they offered embalming and cosmetic services and their establishments became "funeral homes," where the dead could be viewed and funerals held.

Undertakers had the reputation of being indecently eager for business and were accused of encouraging extravagance in the name of a "respectable" funeral. The local undertaker often knew how much the family had received from an insurance company or a burial club—he might even be the secretary of the club—and adjusted his bill accordingly.

> "Undertakers have been known," [the vicar] said, "to offer medical men 10 per cent of the cost of a funeral for supplying early information of the death. Such cases are believed to be comparatively rare. This reservation, however, cannot be extended to insurance agents. The following is typical of what happens almost every day. A father of four children, who was insured for £7 died. The widow informed an undertaker who called at the house that she was unable to make the funeral arrangements until she had received the money. 'Do not let that trouble you,' said the man. 'You can pay when convenient.'
>
> "The widow is still wondering how the cost of the funeral amounted to exactly £7. The secret is that the insurance agent communicated the news of the death and the amount of the policy to the undertaker, at the same time drawing the usual commission for his trouble.
>
> "When the woman returned from the ceremony she had not a penny left in the world, and for long her children have been pinched with the want of food. How long shall these men be allowed to fleece the poor in life and rob them in death?"
>
> —*New Zealand Herald* [Auckland, NZ], 28 October, 1905: p. 2.

Conversely, undertakers often complained of how they were unjustly accused by the public of making fabulous profits on their dismal merchandise, the difficulty of getting paid and of being "stiffed" by their clients.

> "Now, one would think that the bill for the burial of father, mother, sister or brother would be among the first to be paid by surviving relatives. The fact is that the undertaker never expects to collect his bill within six months after the funeral, for the reason that very, very few begin to think of paying before that time. In the case of estates, where the bill goes to executors or administrators, it is sometimes years before the bill is paid. These are the things that make the life of the undertaker unhappy.
>
> "In the meantime," continued the funeral director, "we have to pay up promptly every month our bills for carriages to the livery stable, our coffin bills, our advertising bills and the wages of our help—all have to be met promptly when due. Then there are the horses to be kept, etc. Every undertaker has his hearse and dead wagon and buggy. One concern has three hearses and two dead wagons. People say that the price of coffins, the cost of funerals, is excessive. Considering all things they are very moderate."
>
> "What is the cost of an average, respectable funeral?"
>
> "Well, that all depends. The location of the grave, the number of carriages, etc., regulate the cost. Man or woman, however, can be very nicely buried for $200. That is a good average funeral. But where most of us get a case of that kind we get a number where the price is nothing. You see the undertaker must answer his call without asking any questions. Like the doctor he is summoned and must respond whether there is money in it or not. When people die they must be buried, you know. So you see there is more to make the undertaker gloomy than the mere funeral trappings with which he is surrounded."
>
> —*The San Francisco [CA] Call,* 26 August, 1896: p. 7.

Most undertakers were ethical, conscientious and respected, but there were whispered claims that some were in league with doctors or, worse, with medical schools.

THE PAUPER DEAD SCANDAL

The fact that the city contracts with unscrupulous undertakers to bury the pauper dead at a disgracefully low price has always been productive of scandals. The case of J. Edward Cook, who was practically forced to allow his wife's corpse to go to the dissecting table because he was too poor to pay the contract undertaker $15 for a burial was told in The Star yesterday. It is only one of dozens of just such tricks that have been performed by undertakers who took the contract to bury the poor at a price less than a decent shroud would cost.

Once a city contract undertaker was caught burying the bodies of three pauper children in a soap box. Another time a contract undertaker buried boxes of sand and sold the bodies of persons whose friends had paid for decent funerals to medical colleges for dissection.

—*The Kansas City [MO] Star,* 30 January, 1899: p. 1.

Just as undertakers advertised lady embalmers to care for women and children, the lady undertaker was seen to have a moral and aesthetic advantage over the "man undertaker."

A Lady Undertaker.

Buffalo is blessed with a "lady undertaker," who takes charge of every detail of a funeral, embalming the body, draping the funeral apartments, furnishing the shroud and casket, chairs, and carriages, arranging the flowers, and purchasing the mourning outfit for the entire family. In the latter capacity she has great advantage over the man undertaker, who has vague and unsatisfactory ideas on ruching and borders, doesn't know the fine distinctions in mourning etiquette between the suitable garb for maids and matrons, and is no use whatever in deciding which style in mourning bonnets is most becoming. Many people prefer to have this little woman attend women and children especially, and she is doing a thriving business, which she intends to supplement in the spring by a millinery establishment, from which to supply promptly the requisite costume at short notice....

—*Wheeling [WV] Register,* 7 February, 1892: p. 7.

The rumored collusion between undertakers and doctors made both the target of jokes.

Visitor, to undertaker: "Why are you so sad to-day?"

Undertaker: "I have just buried Dr. Blank."

Visitor: "Ah, indeed! The Doctor was a philanthropical gentleman."

Undertaker: "He was. He threw many a dollar into my hands."

—*The Physicians and Surgeons' Investigator, A Monthly Journal of Medicine and Surgery*, January, 1885: p. 27.

A Reciprocity Treaty

Old Doctor: "I was informed last night that your son and my daughter propose to wed if there is no objection."

Wealthy Undertaker: "So I heard. Good idea ain't it?"

"Think so?"

"Yes; don't you see? It won't matter then whether you lose patients or not, the money will be in the family."

—*Springfield [OH] Daily Republic,* 14 January, 1888: p. 3.

The Last Word

The designation "Funeral Director" emerged in the 1830s, although "undertaker" was the more common name throughout the eighteenth and nineteenth centuries. The term "mortician" was first used in 1895, after the editor of *The Embalmers' Monthly* ran a contest to find a more genteel term to replace "undertaker."

V is for Veil
Sewn out of crape
It hides tear-stained faces
From those who would gape

The mourning veil was a dead giveaway that the wearer was in the deepest of mourning. Made of crape or of crape-edged silk, the mourning veil was worn pinned or tied to a bonnet or hat. It was long and heavy and, depending on the material, it might be nearly opaque.

Many widows commented that not only did it protect them from the prying eyes of the public, it also hid their tears. The mourning veil also alerted strangers that the woman wearing it should be treated with consideration and sympathy. In the literature of fashion, the veil assumed an almost sacred significance.

> A mourning dress does protect the wearer while in deepest grief from the intrusive gayety of a passing stranger—it is a wall, a cell of refuge. Behind a black veil a poor broken-hearted woman can hide herself, as she goes out for business or recreation, dreading lest any one shall speak to her.
>
> —*Harper's Bazaar,* 15 August, 1881: p. 514.

> Of all the inventions of a refined civilization, perhaps there is not one more appropriate and welcome than the widow's veil. Many a stricken woman could not be persuaded to go beyond the threshold of her desolated home but for this welcome screen, which gives her the sacred seclusion she craves, while she moves once more among the busy, indifferent crowd. How she clings to it! How she hesitates to lay it aside, even when her kindly friends remind that her allotted years of such weeds of mourning are over.
>
> —*Godey's Lady's Book,* June, 1863: p. 554.

> A widow, or mother, in the newness of her long veil, has her hard path made as little difficult as possible by everyone with whom she comes in contact, no matter on what errand she may be bent. A clerk in a store will try to wait on her as quickly and as attentively as possible. Acquaintances avoid stopping her with long conversation that could not but torture and distress her. She meets small

> kindnesses at every turn, which save unnecessary jars to supersensitive nerves.
>
> —*Etiquette in Society, in Business, in Politics and at Home.* Emily Post. 1914: p. 399.

Despite these benefits, mourning veils were criticized as a health hazard by doctors, who claimed that women inhaled poisonous chemicals from the fabric, got rashes from the dye, which bled onto the skin, and ruined their eyes peering through the thick cloth.

> The doctors are now inveighing sharply against the black crape veil so generally worn by ladies in mourning. They pronounce it unhealthy, expensive and unbecoming. Dr. Hunter McGuire says: The black crape veil is undoubtedly hurtful, and the custom should be abandoned; apart from its poisonous dye and offensive smell, mechanically it interferes with healthful respiration.
>
> —*The Charlotte [NC] Democrat,* 18 December, 1885: p. 1.

> So many eyes have been injured by the persistent wearing of crape veils, that physicians forbid them. The eyes that survive the bitterness of tears succumb to the poisonous rasping of crape.
>
> —*The Delineator*, October, 1895: p. 493.

These warnings had little effect on the wearers of mourning veils. Etiquette books outlined how the veil should be worn—over the face or thrown back?—and how long for each degree of bereavement. Veils were worn by widows and, depending on the date and the etiquette authority consulted, for the death of a child or parent.

> How long should a very young widow wear a veil over her face, and, after putting the veil back, how long should it be worn?
>
> Six months or a year over the face, and as long as she wishes afterwards, but not less than two years.
>
> —*The Home Manual: Everybody's Guide in Social, Domestic, and Business Life.* Mrs. John A. Logan, *et al.* 1889: p. 74.

The toxicity of crape aside, there were other unpleasant aspects to wearing a mourning veil, some of which hung down to the knee or the heel.

> It is torture of the most acute physical kind to wear crape veils. They pull and rag the head in a way no one could believe unless she wears one, to say nothing of the corpselike odor of the crape when the sun shines on it.
>
> —*The Sunday Leader* [Wilkes-Barre, PA], 10 September, 1899: p. 16.

> Nor do I believe in two years of sable gloom and enforced solitude. Look at the dismal figures seen every day on the street, in cars, in church, swathed in hopeless black, the faces even entirely shrouded by a long, heavy $15 or $20 veil, shutting out sunshine and air, dangerous to eyes, complexion and health, and giving every passer-by a chill. If one ventures, after months of torture, to throw back the veil, how it drags off the bonnet, pulling down the hair, piercing the head with pins askew, and the unhappy being is jerked about until the neck is nearly dislocated by those who are trying to get by.
>
> —*New York [NY] Tribune,* 14 March, 1889: p. 7.

> "Physicians, you know, have always cried out against the wearing of crape. They declare it to be one of the worst things possible for a grief stricken mind. The very weight of a heavy crape veil is enough to depress one. And," she added, dropping her voice confidentially, "I don't mind telling you they are the very worst things to manage. Why, at first I couldn't get a veil long enough or thick enough, I was so miserable. But the first time I ventured out into a street car with my long veil settled it. I caught it in the door when I entered, and as I seated myself nearly jerked my bonnet off my head. The conductor released the veil, and as I prepared to gather it about me a fat woman put her foot through it, and a horrid young man opposite grinned.
>
> —*Kansas City [MO] Times,* 16 October, 1885: p. 4.

Widows were too often the subject of cruel jokes implying that their sorrow could be solaced by fashion.

> Dressmaker (to bereaved widow): "How long would you like the mourning veil to be, madam?"
>
> Bereaved widow (with a burst of grief): "I don't care for expense at a time like this; my husband's death was a dreadful blow. Make the veil as long as style will warrant."
>
> —*Grip* [Toronto, Ontario], 25 February, 1888: p. 10.

> The widow's veil isn't always a vale of tears.
>
> —*Auckland [NZ] Star*, 27 April, 1901: p. 2.

The Last Word

There seems to be no 19th-century documentation indicating that mourning veils were ever called "weeping veils," although they were occasionally called "weepers." The term "weeping veil" appeared in a short story in 1910. Its next appearance was in 1912, in an article by Dorothy Dix, about some of the "idiotic conventions" of wearing mourning. Black lace veils for mourning were advertised, but they are never mentioned in etiquette books and lace is specifically prohibited in first mourning. That does not mean lace was not worn; there was more variation in actual mourning wear than the etiquette books would have us believe.

W is for weepers
Tied round the top hat
To cover the shine
All mourning is matte

Weepers were the male equivalent of the mourning veil and consisted of a band or scarf of crape tied around the base of the top hat and hanging down behind. The long crape streamers fluttered from mourners' hats like crape from a door knob—the badge of bereavement hung to signal a house of mourning, which was also called a weeper.

> Perhaps no people in the world *exhibit* more regret for their dead than the Americans. When death becomes a guest in any family his presence there—if seeking the old—is announced by a long black weeper fastened to the lintels of the entrance doors. If a child has been summoned hence, the weepers are black and white, tied together with white or black bows....In many places the weepers remain on the windows or doors for months.
>
> —*New Zealand Herald* [Auckland, NZ], 6 February, 1875: p. 3.

Weepers were meant to cover the silk or plush hat's shiny finish, providing the dull finish required for mourning. While Victorian women in mourning were clothed from head to toe in black, widowers were only required to show their mourning on hat or sleeve.

> Mr. [Thomas George] Webster's other picture, *Alone,* represents an old man in a dark smock frock, sitting alone by the cold hearth of his cottage, just returned from his wife's funeral....His hat, covered with a great crape weeper, just taken off, lies on the table beside him...from which, with help of the black cotton gloves thrown down by it...it pours...a sense of crape and funerals into the mind, from which one passes next to the lonely old man whom it oppresses.
>
> —*The Examiner* [London, England], 2 May, 1863: p. 8.

Weepers were worn by undertakers, mutes, and other participants in large public funerals like the drivers of hearses and mourners' carriages.

> Their drivers sit very high up with a black velvet pall across their throne-like perches. Their crape weepers flow down their backs from one to two yards from their hats.
>
> —*The Wichita [KS] Eagle,* 6 August, 1887: p. 7.

> Surely, heart-felt grief for those who have gone does not need to find expression in black crape and broadcloth, hideous 'mourning carriages,' coal-black horses, a hearse of more or less fanciful design bedecked with bunches of black feathers, and a lot of hired mourners with crape 'weepers' round their hats, and suits of sombre black.
>
> —*The New Zealand Observer and Free Lance* [Auckland, NZ], 1 June, 1895: p. 2.

> The members of the council walked two and two, wearing crape weepers, and led by the mayor....They were attended by the corporation liveried officials, wearing crape hat-bands. Then followed in a long double line the members of the Masonic lodges of Kilkenny. The members mustered nearly a hundred in number, and wore crape weepers, and the usual emblematic blue ribbon badge in the buttonhole.
>
> —*The Freeman's Journal* [Dublin, Ireland], 5 October, 1854: p. 3.

The term weepers was also used more widely to describe other signs of mourning, including a widow's collar and cuffs, the lappets of a widow's cap, or mourning sleeve bands.

> The great black crape "weeper" tied to the left arm is no longer seen except among the sincere poor. Nor is the band of crape worn upon the sleeve, except as an officially prescribed token of respect to some deceased member of a military or civic organization to which the wearer belongs.
>
> —*The Delineator*, October, 1895: p. 493.

The Last Word

Weepers are different from a mourning hatband, which was often made of black bombazine and fit only around the hat, while weepers are made of crape and are designed to trail behind. Weepers and hat bands were listed as separate items in mourning advertisements.

X for the Sexton
Who buries the masses
He taps swelling coffins
For flammable gases

The gravedigger or sexton, as he or she was called in England and in some parts of the United States, dug graves, carried coffins and lowered them into the grave, monitored burials in vaults, and might serve as a graveyard watchman to keep away body snatchers.

In England's larger cities, the dead were traditionally buried in churchyards—cemeteries attached to a church and run by the parish. Due to a lack of space, graves were reused in these burial grounds. Sextons and gravediggers would, after a certain time had elapsed, shovel up corpses and coffins, skulls, and bones to be burned in the "bone house," where tools were kept and bodies were sometimes held in winter if the ground was too hard to dig a grave.

Before germ theory was introduced in the late nineteenth century, many people believed disease was transmitted via noxious odors, which gave rise to fears of disease from half-decayed corpses and their offensive smells. The gases released by decomposition could also cause a lead coffin to swell and even burst open. It was the job of the sexton to drill a small hole and light off the gasses of swelling coffins to prevent them from exploding. Sextons and gravediggers were reputed to drink heavily to cope with this and other difficult aspects of the job.

> "TAPPING" COFFINS.—It is well known to those engaged in burying the dead, that when leaden coffins are employed, the expansive force of the gas, and the consequent bulging out of the coffin, compels the workmen frequently to "tap" it, that the gas may escape. The "tapping" is performed by boring a hole with a gimlet; a jet of gas instantly passes through the aperture, and this, when ignited, produces a flame that lasts from ten minutes to half an hour. The men who perform this operation are perfectly aware of the risk they encounter, and they are extremely careful how they execute it.
>
> —*The Era* [London, England], 15 December, 1839: p. 4.

> A grave-digger is asked respecting what is called the "tapping" of leaden coffins, and he replied that he would not object to do it; "if you keep underneath the coffin you would not have so much

> of the gas then, if you keep underneath the gas flies up, if you tap it underneath, if there is any dead water or 'soup' as it is called, it runs into a pail, and then it is taken and thrown into some place or another, perhaps down a gully-hole. I have been compelled before now to put my clothes out of the window, because the stench has been so great they could not bear the place."
>
> —*The Morning Chronicle* [London, England], 26 August, 1842: p. 3.

Gaseous coffins were not the only hazard a sexton faced. This sexton found the grave to be a fine and private place where a fellow might find himself embraced.

> A grave-digger at St. Anne's, Soho, says, "I dug a grave on a Sunday evening, on purpose to get ready for Monday; it rained that Sunday evening; and when I went to work on Monday morning, I finished my work, and I was trying the length of the grave to see if it was long enough and wide enough, so that I should not have to go down again; and while I was in there the ground gave way, and a body turned right over, and the two arms came and clasped me round the neck; she had gloves on, and stockings, and white flannel inside, and what we call a shift, but no head." This horrible circumstance the witness accounts for, by supposing that his predecessor in the office of gravedigger had stripped the body of its coffin, and had also carried away the head for the purposes of dissection; and that the body, being left near the surface, fell on him when the earth gave way.
>
> —*The Morning Chronicle* [London, England], 26 August, 1842: p. 3.

Spending time with the dead and the decaying inclined many sextons to melancholy and superstition.

> "Gravedigging is not a gay business," said a gravedigger, "but it is a very old one, and many curious superstitions surround it. One of these is never to buy a new spade. To dig a grave with a spade that is new is supposed to bring death in the family within a twelve-month. Hence gravediggers buy their spades second hand as a

rule. Another superstition with some is that a grave should never stand open overnight. It should not, they say, be dug till the day of the funeral. If it is made the day before, beware. There is a third superstition that if a cock crows once while a grave is being dug one friend of the digger will die; if it crows twice, two will die; if thrice, three."

—*Arizona Republican* [Phoenix, AZ], 20 July, 1906: p. 4.

Sextons and gravediggers also monitored coffins in vaults to make sure that bodies and grave goods were not stolen. However, some supplemented their income by preying on the dead, both by helping body snatchers (See RESURRECTION MEN) or theft. One sexton was arrested with a collection of hundreds of burial garments that he'd stolen over a period of nine years. Jewelry and other valuables placed in coffins were also at risk from unscrupulous sextons.

A Sexton, having the management of a small Ground in London, had many burials, and yet never filled up the ground; for his constant practice was to sell the bodies, burn the wood of the coffins, reserving the handles and plates for old metal. He carried on a regular trade, and at night coaches were frequently seen fetching the bodies away from his house.

—*The Present Scandalous System of Robbing Graves Exposed: And a Safeguard for the Dead, Now Presented to the British Public in the Newly Invented Iron or Metallic Coffins, Tablets and Tombs.* Royal Patent Burial Company. 1818: p. 30.

Although it was a lonely job, honest sextons were prepared for intruders.

WALKING ARSENALS.

Some Methods Employed By Sextons and Watchman.

In their midnight prowlings about the grave-yards the sextons and watchmen go armed to the teeth with revolvers and often times with guns. Dogs are a necessary adjunct of a cemetery, and from three to ten are always kept.

Several sextons and watchmen say that as soon as they hear the least noise they always fire their revolvers. As long as they have their revolvers and dogs by them they are not afraid of men or ghosts. Indeed, it would not be safe for any one to prowl around a grave-yard of this city.

Sextons say that they are never afraid of running across thieves hiding in the grave-yards at night, because any one with a guilty conscience is always superstitious and gives graveyards a wide berth.

—*The Cincinnati [OH] Enquirer*, 31 January, 1892: p. 9.

Like the gravedigger in *Hamlet*, the sexton was often possessed of a grave sense of humor.

An Illinois grave-digger, who buried a man named Button, sent his widow the following bill: "To making one button hole, $2.50."

—*The Jackson [OH] Standard*, 16 May, 1878: p. 1.

Old Lady: This must be a very healthy place. Now, what may the death rate be?

Grave-Digger: Wonderful steady, Mum; wonderful steady. Just one death to each person right along.

—*Sketch*, 21 July, 1897: p. 537.

The Last Word

There were female sextons, although most of them, like Hester Hammerton [1711-1746], sexton of All Saints, Kingston upon Thames, inherited the position from their father or took over their husband's job. Examples of women sextons included Elizabeth Thorn, [1832-1907] "The Angel of Gettysburg," and "Mrs Kitchener," seen in photographs in the collections of the Imperial War Museum, carrying on her husband's gravedigging at Aley Green Cemetery, Luton, while he was serving in the First World War.

Y is for churchyard

O'erflowing with death

Scents and miasmas

Make one hold one's breath

In Victorian England the dead did not always rest in peace. The traditional burial place was a plot of consecrated land surrounding the parish church, called the churchyard or, in Scotland, the kirkyard. In many churchyards, after a decent interval of five to ten years, the grave would be reused. In a small village, the churchyard was not normally overwhelmed by large numbers of burials. However, in large cities, the churchyards were packed to capacity. The newspapers and health commissioners' reports were full of horror stories about stenches and disease from decaying flesh and coffins resurfacing, either from being buried less than six feet under or by careless shovel work by gravediggers. City churchyards had become death traps. [See SEXTON.]

It was a very real fear of those who lived near churchyards that the dreadful odors were the cause of disease.

> CHURCHYARD FEVER.—The neighbourhood of the Hampstead-road has been visited for some time past with a frightful outbreak of fever, which got the name of "The Churchyard Fever," and other destructive diseases that have carried off numbers of the inhabitants living near St. James Chapel churchyard— young children being the principal victims. Mr. Day, surgeon, of Robert-street, attributes this wholesale decimation to the foul malaria arising from the graveyard, which he described at an inquest held before Mr. Wakely last week on a child that died from debility, consequent on the foul state of the atmosphere of that vicinity, as a complete mass of human putrefaction. Although the graveyard (said Mr. Day) only comprised three acres, it had beneath its surface upwards of 60,000 corpses, some of the coffins only having a slight covering of earth; and at night a column of thick miasma laden with disease and death might be seen arising from this field of corruption, poisoning the surrounding atmosphere. Mr. Day clearly traced the unhealthy condition of the inhabitants to the abominable graveyard exhalations which covered the walls of the beadle's[2] dwelling situated in the churchyard with a thick coating of sulphuretted hydrogen

[2] The unfortunate beadle mentioned in this story was an English parish official, often responsible for overseeing charitable works.

gas. A short time back he attended the beadle's family, all of whom were suffering from fever, of which the beadle died, while his son was now sinking from consumption. Even the Rev. Dr. Stebbings, while performing divine service in the chapel, fainted, and had to be carried out in that state. The former gravedigger was attacked with cholera, and narrowly escaped death, after digging a grave, which he was unable to finish in consequence of the stench. Mr. Day has often explained to the trustees the dangers arising from this graveyard, yet burials are still allowed there, and as many as twenty-three have taken place in it on one Sunday. Unless this graveyard is immediately closed and concreted over, Mr. Day is of [the] opinion that in the warm weather it will be the seat of another outbreak of cholera or some other equally frightful disease.

—*The Morning Chronicle* [London, England], 27 June, 1853: p. 8.

London was not the only large city with deadly churchyards.

**CITY CEMETERIES.
A MASS OF TESTIMONY TO
SHOW THEIR UNHEALTHFULNESS**

Dr. Barton in his report on the yellow fever in New Orleans in 1853 says that the greatest mortality obtained in the district where the principal cemeteries were located declares "that in no case should a dwelling be permitted within several hundred yards of a cemetery," and recommends that "all cemeteries within city limits be closed against future use." Dr. Bryant writing on yellow fever at Norfolk in 1855, also regards the city cemeteries as a constant source of danger in an epidemic and urges "the total forbidding of intra-mural or even near by suburban cemeteries." When the fever was in New York in 1822 the report of the board of health showed that the mortality in the vicinity of Trinity church graveyard was as three to one when compared with any other portions of the city....This churchyard was the center of the very fatal prevalence of cholera at every visit of that pest from 1832 to 1854....

Dr. Ranch, of Iowa, writes that during the prevalence of the cholera in Burlington in 1850 "there were no deaths in the neighborhood of the cemetery until some twenty had been buried there. Afterward, until the epidemic ceased, cases were constant, and always in the direction from the cemetery in which the wind blew."

Buck in his Hygiene, writes: "It is impossible for any one to say how long the materies morbi may continue to live under ground. If organic matter can be broiled and frozen without losing its vitality, and seeds 3,000 years old will sprout when planted, it would be hardihood to assert that the poison of cholera, or small pox, or typhus may not for years lie dormant, but not dead in the moist temperature of the grave."

—*Daily Honolulu [HI] Press*, 24 March, 1886: p. 1.

A cholera epidemic in 1849 overwhelmed London's churchyards. The 1852 Metropolitan Burial Act closed these cemeteries to burials and parish Burial Boards bought land for what would become the "Magnificent Seven" cemeteries: St Pancras and Islington Cemetery, Norwood, Brompton, Highgate, Nunhead, Abney Park, and Tower Hamlets. Rural or "garden" cemeteries also were established, far from city centers, and with ample room for new burials. [See NECROPOLIS.] They were meant to be scenic, park-like, and open to the public.

The design of these rural Cemeteries was to remove from the last resting places of the friends loved and lost that gloom and dread.... It was to give our bodies a holier resting place, where brighter aspects are presented to the survivors."

—*The Cincinnati Cemetery of Spring Grove: Report for 1857.*
Spring Grove Cemetery (Cincinnati, Ohio). 1857: pp. 3-4.

A censorious Englishman on a tour of North America commented on the differences between city churchyards and a garden cemetery.

After an early dinner, we drove out of the town to the Grave-yard, one of the prettiest burying places I ever saw. It occupies an area of twenty acres, laid out in avenues, and divided by rows of trees into lots for the different inhabitants. These connecting lanes or roads are not gravelled, but laid down in grass, as well as the intermediate spaces, which are spotted over with handsome monuments of all sizes and forms, giving a lively instead of a gloomy air, to the whole scene....

There is certainly some improvement in this, compared with... a soppy churchyard, where the mourners sink ankle-deep in a rank and offensive mould, mixed up with broken bones and fragments of coffins; or that the cause of virtue is advanced by the recollection of coughs, colds, and rheumatisms...caught whilst half a dozen old fellows, with long-tailed, threadbare black coats, are filling up a grave, for which they themselves might seem the readiest tenants.

—*Travels in North America, in the Years 1827 and 1828*, Vol. 2.
Basil Hall. 1830: p. 201.

The Last Word

The first garden cemetery in the United States was Mt. Auburn in Cambridge, Massachusetts, established in 1831. By the late 1830s, it had become a popular tourist attraction. A guidebook, *The Picturesque Pocket Companion and Visitor's Guide Through Mt. Auburn*, described its monuments and notable burials.

Z is for zinc

"White Bronze" as it's known

It lasts so much longer

Than crumbling stone

It is easy to recognize a White Bronze monument among a field of pink or grey granite tombstones—it will have a sharpness of outline like nothing else in the cemetery. The inscriptions are crystal clear, as if cast yesterday.

White Bronze was the trade name of a metal used to make tombstones and monuments. It was not actually white or bronze. The material is pure zinc and is a distinctive bluish-grey color. The name "White Bronze" was chosen to express its durability and artistic quality. The inventor, Milo Amos Richardson, superintendent of the Sherman Cemetery in Sherman, New York, was distressed by how quickly stone monuments weathered and decayed. After experimenting with several other materials, he chose zinc. Parts of each monument were sand cast, then the pieces were bonded together with liquid zinc poured into the joints. It was much cheaper to cast names and epitaphs on plaques for a monument than it would be to have the same text carved in stone.

Richardson's original company failed because he couldn't find a foundry experienced in working with pure zinc. The process was eventually perfected and the Monumental Bronze Company of Bridgeport, Connecticut and its subsidiaries sold monuments around the country from the 1870s up to the 1930s. Rather than display the tombstones in showrooms, their agents sold the markers from lavishly illustrated catalogues showing the company's many different designs, which could be mixed and matched to create a uniquely personal monument. Sample monuments in miniature were also made for agents to show to customers.

Prices ranged from $2.50 for a bouquet holder to $300 for a three-quarters-sized angel to $1,450 for a life-sized statue of a soldier. They also offered a two-foot-high "Marker for the millions" for a budget-friendly $16.00. The public's taste for elaborate monuments began to decline after the First World War. The Bridgeport Monumental Bronze factory closed in 1939.

White Bronze/zinc monuments are still frequently seen in cemeteries and unless the metal has buckled, their seams have weakened, or someone has removed the text plaques, they usually look as fresh as the day they were set up. There are online communities of enthusiasts for "zinkies" as the monuments are affectionately called.

The company was not shy about shouting the advantages of their product in all caps.

> Our Bronze is composed of Pure Cast Zinc, which differs materially from the commercial article, being REFINED especially for our own use, and it is also an entirely different article from sheet zinc, which is an amalgam, whilst ours is a PURE METAL, like gold, silver and copper; and for information as to the ENDURING NATURE of this metal, please consult the STANDARD WORKS ON METALLURGY as well as the testimonials of acknowledged scientists.
>
> The beautiful surface finish on all our work is produced by the PATENTED "SAND BLAST" PROCESS, of which we have the exclusive control for this class of work, and by means of which we impart a finish closely resembling granite, and the material (being of a LIGHT GRAY COLOR) is more pleasing to the eye in the form of STATUES and MONUMENTS than is the DARK or ANTIQUE BRONZE (which is an amalgam of zinc, tin and copper), and this improvement in finish and color justly entitles our goods to their TRADE NAME of "White Bronze."
>
> —*Catalogue of The Monumental Bronze Co., Bridgeport, Connecticut, U.S.A.*, October, 1882, p. 1.

SOME OF THE ADVANTAGES IN FAVOR OF THE WHITE BRONZE FOR MONUMENTS, STATUES, &c.

1st.—Age will not impair their beauty.

2d.—There being no deterioration in their value, you always have in these your money's worth; while, with marble, or even granite, what you obtained at great expense, may, in a few years, become of little or no value, as defective headstones and monuments in every cemetery bear witness...

3d.—Our designs are far more elaborate and beautiful than can be made in stone at double the cost.

> 4th.—Beautiful Bas-relief emblems, full of meaning, can be selected from our large list of models, and cast solidly on the monuments without any additional cost.
>
> 5th.—The most delicate lines and sharpest letters will not chip nor lose a particle of their beauty.
>
> 6th.—The inscriptions, without additional expense, are all in raised letters which cannot be broken off, while the action of the frost and constant disintegration on letters of stone ultimately obliterate them.
>
> By means of removable tablets our monuments can be made to present a finished appearance at all times, with no blank tablets, for each one can be filled with inscriptions, mottoes, or emblems at time of erection, without extra cost, and then be removed at any time when circumstances require additional inscriptions to occupy their places. This pleasing feature is not available in stone work...
>
> We now feel that we can truthfully and conscientiously say, without fear or favor, and prove it by scientific facts, as well as historical data, that the White Bronze Monuments and Statues are the BEST IN THE WORLD....
>
> —*Catalogue of The Monumental Bronze Co., Bridgeport, Connecticut, U.S.A.*, October, 1882, p. 2.

Sellers of traditional stone tombstones countered white bronze's aggressive advertising by lobbying to have zinc monuments banned by cemeteries and sowing doubt with notices like this one:

> **DON'T BE HUMBUGGED.**
>
> There are parties traveling through the county offering for sale what they call a white bronze monument, which is nothing but galvanized iron. They will show you some very nice samples, which look well, but the monuments are but a thin shell filled with gravel, to give them weight, and which in a few years will turn black. Look out for them. There is nothing equals Marble, or Granite, that has stood the test for ages. L. ROOT & Co.
>
> —*Washington [KS] Register*, 1 April, 1892: p. 1.

The Last Word

White bronze manufacturers created identical "Silent Sentinel" Civil War monuments for North and South communities, merely changing the initials on the soldier's belt buckle to represent the Union or the Confederate States. The company also offered the ultimate in personalization.

> When used as a Family Monument, and photos of the deceased soldier can be furnished, we will model a new head in a true likeness of said deceased, thus bringing out a complete portrait statue, and the extra cost will be but $150, thus giving to the public full life-sized portrait soldier statues at a cost of only $600. This will enable many families to mark their soldier graves, independent of the tardy movements of the public in this direction.
>
> —*Catalogue of The Monumental Bronze Co., Bridgeport, Connecticut, U.S.A.*, October, 1882, p. 85.

Appendix
Etiquette of Mourning Dress

There is much variation in the times required for mourning, depending on the decade, the authority consulted, and the closeness of the relation being mourned. In addition to familial relations, in the United States when a notable person died, it was standard that mourning be worn for thirty days. In England, Court Mourning of varying lengths was declared periodically for royalty at home and abroad.

1838

Mourning is worn for a husband or wife, from one to two years.

For a parent, six months or a year.

For children, if above ten years old, from six months to a year; below that age, from three to six months; for an infant, six weeks and upwards.

For brothers and sisters, six to eight months.

For uncles and aunts, three to six months.

For cousins, or uncles and aunts, related by marriage, from six weeks to three months.

For more distant relations or friends, from three weeks upwards.

—*The Workwoman's Guide.* A Lady.
London, UK: Simpkin, Marshall, and Co. 1838: pp. 121-124.

1860

There is such a variety of opinion upon the subject of mourning, that it is extremely difficult to lay down any general rules upon the subject. Some wear very close black for a long period, for a distant relative; whilst others will wear dressy mourning for a short time in a case of death in the immediate family. There is no rule either for the depth of mourning, or the time when it may be laid aside....

—*Ladies' Book of Etiquette, and Manual of Politeness.* Florence Hartley. Boston, Massachusetts: G.W. Cottrell. 1860: p. 32.

1871

The servants are ordinarily put in mourning, by those who can afford it, on the death of an important member of the family. The nurse only in the case of the death of young children.

—*Fashion: The Power That Influences the World.* George P. Fox. New York, New York: American News. 1871: p. 68.

1874

Fashionable Mourning in London.

To commence with the deepest mourning—that of a widow. The dress is... entirely covered with crape... and deep lawn cuffs and a lawn collar are worn. The distinctive cap is worn for a year and a day...After a year, silk heavily trimmed with crape, may be worn for six months, after which the crape may be lightened considerably, and jet trimmings are admissible; after nine months, plain black can be worn. After two years, mourning can be laid aside, but it is better taste to wear half mourning for some months....

The next degree of mourning is that of children for their parents, which is of the same duration as that of parents for a child—namely, one year. For three months, paramatta [fine wool and cotton fabric] or some similar material, heavily trimmed with crape, should be worn with lawn collars and cuffs; for the next three, silk, with slightly less crape, the same collars and cuffs. After six months, crape is laid aside, and plain black worn for one month; black ornaments and gloves must be worn, after which gold, diamonds, silver, pearls and grey gloves sewn with black are admissible. After nine months, half mourning is quite correct. No society should be indulged in for two months; after that ordinary habits may be gradually resumed; but crape is out of place at balls, so they should be avoided while it is worn....In the case of a man who has lost his first wife and married again, it is customary, if either of the parents of the first wife die, for the second wife to wear slight mourning for three months, more especially if there should be any children by the first marriage; this is not compulsory, but it is usual, and in good taste. The second wife, however, is not expected to wear mourning for any of the other relatives of her predecessor.

—*The Western Daily Press* [Bristol, Avon, UK], 19 August, 1874: p. 4.

1888

Fashions change as to mourning, though less frequently and radically than in other dress. According to the newest usage in New York society, very deep mourning, such as worn by widows, necessitates not only black and crape, but absolute change of form. The mantle is discarded for a long black cashmere or merino shawl, while a long crape veil must float from her widow's chapeau. Deep mourning [for a widow] lasts a year, during which the long veil and crape trimmings are worn.

When the mourning of the family is deep, say for husband and father, it lasts a year, and is followed by three to six months of half mourning. During the three last months any fancy materials in black can be worn.

Mourning for sisters, brothers, grandparents, etc., lasts nine months, six of these being deep, but less so than for nearer relatives. Woolen crepon, grenadine, embroidered crape, any seasonable black woolen material can be worn, trimmed with crape, but not extensively.

Little ones, even for deep mourning, wear white, but, if old enough to wear colors, black must replace the white— black without crape, the hat being of straw or felt, trimmed with ribbon. After five, little girls wear crape trimmings for a mother or father.

—*The Saint Paul [MN] Globe,* 22 January, 1888: p. 12.

1890

In America, society has not laid down any very strict rules, but the following are those sanctioned by the best authorities and the usage of society.

For a Husband: the usual period of mourning is two years, although it is sometimes shortened to one....

For a Wife. The widower wears mourning for one year in America, and two years in England....

For Parents. The period of mourning is one year for parents....

For Grand-Parents. The rule is the same as for parents in America, but in England this mourning only lasts three months.

For Brothers and Sisters. For these the period of mourning is one year....

For Children. For those above ten years of age mourning lasts nine months....

For younger children mourning is worn from three to six months. For an infant, six or seven weeks is the usual time.

For Uncles, Aunts and Cousins. For these the period of mourning is from three to six months. When these are relatives by marriage only, from six weeks to three months is considered long enough....

For Nephews and Nieces: For these the mourning is the same as for an uncle or aunt.

For a relative who leaves you an inheritance, the mourning is the same as for a grand-parent.

—*Modern Manners and Social Forms: A Manual of the Manners and Customs of the Best Modern Society*. Mrs. Julia M. Bradley. Chicago, Illinois: James Bethuel Smiley. 1889, pp. 135-136.

1892

The widower, and the man wearing the [mourning hat] band for father or mother should wear it unaltered for at least a year; after that period, according to individual taste, it may be lowered.

The same rule holds good for the band worn for brother or sister, one year being the proper duration of deep mourning.

For aunts, uncles, cousins and collateral relations the period varies from three to six months, according to the degree of intimacy and affection existing between the dead and bereaved.

In "complimentary" mourning, a ghastly term used to denote that worn for parents-in-law, the rule is the same as for the closer and truer kinship.

The mourning for parents-in-law is, however, purely arbitrary and depends principally upon how much they leave. The bigger the bank account the deeper the mourning, especially for mothers-in-law. Any man, however, who honors his wife will show her deceased parents the same respect he would his own, and nothing could possibly appear in worse taste than to see a woman in all the trappings of woe, while her husband disregards the custom entirely.

—*Repository* [Canton, OH], 30 July, 1892: p. 12.

1895

As for mourning for children, it was not worn at all formerly. For some years past it has become the custom to wear it, but only for one's own children. It is worn for six or twelve months, according to the age of the child which has died.

With regard to mourning worn by children, it should be white up to 6 years of age. Children above 8 years should be dressed in black, gray, or black and white, but less severely than grownup persons.

—*Wilkes-Barre [PA] Times Leader*, 5 July, 1895: p. 6.

1900

A widow wears her weeds for 12 months and is seldom seen during the first half year except at church. At the expiration of the year she introduces for six months a little white into her garb....The fancy of the moment is not for very long veils, those reaching to within a few inches of the waist being most in vogue, although Paris advocates long streamer effects which sweep with the train. This may be regarded as the extreme of fashion and not in general favor.

After 18 months it is merely a matter of fancy whether the wearing of mourning in its kindred stages—meaning mauves, gray and violet—shall be discarded altogether or if one shall resume the wearing of colors. Age usually settles the point. A very young widow will undoubtedly take advantage of the latitude thus allowed and emerge from her period of sackcloth and ashes in raiment of brightest hue....

—*The Buffalo [NY] Times,* 7 January, 1900: p. 3.

1901

The widow who purposes to leave off her mourning in due time wears a crape bonnet and long veil and crape-trimmed gowns a year. After this black costumes of crape de chine, lusterless silk, etc., are assumed, with hats and bonnets garnished with black ribbon and black flowers, black chiffon, and dull jet ornaments. After six months, white and lilac touches may suitably relieve the second mourning; and after two years have expired, colors may be resumed....It is not wise nor in good taste to put children under fifteen years of age in mourning, and no girl under seventeen should wear crape....

MOURNING TO BE WORN BY MEN.

A widower wears mourning one year or perhaps eighteen months. For first mourning, complete suits of black, white linen, black lusterless silk neckties, dull black leather shoes, black gloves, cuff-links of black enamel, and hat with crape are the rule. The extremely wide hat-band, like the widow's veil that sweeps the floor, is entirely out of favor.

After eight months or a year, the band is wisely put off. For second mourning, if it is adopted, gray or black clothes, black and black-and-white silk neckties, gray gloves, and white, or black and white, linen are the proper articles. Men do not, as a rule, carry black-bordered handkerchiefs.

A gentleman wears mourning for parent, child, sister, or brother six months or a year, as he prefers. The crape hat-band is adopted for this uniform of woe, but narrower than that worn by a widower. Few men wear any mourning for grandparents, cousins, uncles, or aunts; but when they do, second mourning is proper.

—*The New Century Perfect Speaker: A Complete Encyclopedia of Elocution, Oratory and Etiquette.* John Coulter. Chicago, Illinois: Sprague Wholesale Company. 1901: p. 495.

1908

How long should mourning be worn for parents, both having passed away at the same time? J.H.

In case of double bereavement one naturally feels inclined to wear black, at least, half again as long. Mourning is usually worn for a parent for one year; the deepest for six months, then all black the last six. In the present case I should say deep mourning, which implies crape trimmings, for at least a year; then lighter for six months longer.

—*St. Louis [MO] Globe-Democrat*, 28 June, 1908: p. 59.

1909

MOURNING ETIQUETTE

A widow may resume her society life after the first month of her widowhood has expired, in so far as paying calls is concerned, and after two months she may attend small informal gatherings and concerts. When three months have expired she may accept and give invitations to small dinners. This is the modern seclusion, but elderly women frequently make a compromise between the short and the long seclusion, and do not accept or give invitations until six months have expired....[Y]oung girls still in the schoolroom, of ages from ten to fourteen, are not expected to wear black longer than three months, and to go into half mourning at the expiration of that time, commencing with black and white, followed by grays and half mourning shades. Little children are not put into mourning, but wear white with black trimmings.

—*The Brooklyn [NY] Daily Eagle,* 18 April, 1909: p. 16.

1910 French

Deep Mourning

Widow: A year and six months. The year in dull fabrics and *Crêpe anglais.*

The last six months in fancy black fabrics and silks.

For Father, Mother, Father-in-Law, Mother-in-Law: A year and three months. Nine months in crape. The balance in half-mourning.

For an Infant: Worn for six months or one year, depending on the age of the child. In general, if the child is aged 7 or older, the mourning is the same as for a parent.

For Grandfather, Grandmother, Brother, Sister: Six months in crape; six months in fancy black fabrics and silks.

For Uncle and Aunt: Six months. Three months in crape; three months in half-mourning.

1913

The Correct Mourning.

There is a tendency nowadays to curtail the mourning period and to wear deep mourning only for funeral services. Persons who have considered the effect of strict mourning attire on the mind, on the natures of children especially, have departed from strict black and are using gray, black and white or lavender. But for the majority of women the accepted rules regarding dress are still observed....The widow wears her full mourning for a year. After this the crape is omitted, but she still wears black crape de chine, lusterless silks, dull jet and black chiffon.

When six months of this have passed the white and black, gray and lilac shades are worn. When two years have passed colors may be resumed.

For a child a married woman should wear just the same mourning for a year as she does for a husband....A mother does not wear mourning for very young babies. Indeed, the question of wearing black when there are little children in the family has been decided in favor of discarding mourning....Crape ought not to be worn by young girls. Six months is the time for mourning in this case. After this white, white and black, gray and lavender should be worn. There is a tendency to wear white in the summer time, which insures comfort and is rapidly becoming the accepted style for young women.

—*The Herald* [New Orleans, LA], 10 July, 1913: p. 8.

1918

In France, etiquette prescribes mourning for a husband for one year and six weeks; six months of deep mourning, six of ordinary, and six weeks of half mourning.

For a wife, a father, or a mother, six months—three deep and three half mourning.

For a grandparent, two months and a half of slight mourning.

For a brother or a sister, two months, one of which is in deep mourning.

For an uncle or an aunt, three weeks of ordinary black.

In America, with no fixity of rule, ladies have been known to go into deepest mourning for their own relatives or those of their husband, or for people, perhaps, whom they have never seen, and have remained as gloomy monuments of bereavement for seven or ten years, constantly in black; then, on losing a child or a relative dearly loved, they have no extremity of dress left to express the real grief which fills their lives—no deeper black to go into.

—*Manners and Social Usages.* Mary Elizabeth Wilson Sherwood.
New York: Harper & Brothers Publishers, 1918: pp. 252-253.

Glossary

Banshee: A female spirit who knocks or screams to warn of an impending death.

Beadle: An English parish official, often responsible for overseeing the workhouse or charitable works.

Bombazine: A twilled or corded fabric made of silk or of silk and wool, used almost exclusively for mourning clothing.

British Currency: Until 1971 British currency was calculated as pounds (£), shillings (s.) and pence (d.). There were 12 pennies to the shilling, also known as a "bob," and 20 shillings to the pound.

Burial Club: A benevolent or "friendly" society where members paid a small sum each week or month to cover funeral expenses for a husband, wife, child, or other family member. It was claimed that unnatural parents enrolled children in multiple burial clubs so that they could collect a large sum when the neglected child died or was murdered.

Burial in Woollen Acts: Acts of the Parliament of England passed between 1666-1680, requiring all corpses (except paupers and those who died of plague) to be buried in shrouds made of pure English wool. The Acts were meant to stimulate the English wool trade. The family of the deceased would be fined £5 if they did not comply. A family member might "inform" the authorities about the violation so they were able to claim half of the fine back as a reward. The Acts were mostly ignored from the late eighteenth century until they were repealed in 1814.

Casket / Coffin: Both are containers for a dead body. The coffin is six-sided and tapers towards the foot. The casket is rectangular. The term "casket" began to be used in the 1840s and was euphemistically meant to imply a case for a precious jewel: the loved one's corpse. "Casket" is primarily used in the United States, while "coffin" was and is the prevailing term in Britain and Ireland.

Catafalque: A bier or stand, usually elaborately decorated, for holding a coffin or body as it lies in state.

Cholera: A deadly disease spread by a water-borne bacterium. It could cause death within hours. The victim's skin darkened from dehydration so the disease was sometimes called the "black plague," although it is not related to the Bubonic Plague/Black Death. There were numerous cholera outbreaks and five global cholera pandemics in the nineteenth century.

Church of England: The official state church of England, headed by the monarch and the Archbishop of Canterbury. The Church is divided into 42 dioceses, each of which has a cathedral and is presided over by a bishop. Within each diocese are local parishes, consisting of a church and its community. The parish priest, known as the vicar or rector, is responsible for running the parish jointly with a council of representatives elected from the congregation.

Coffin Furniture: Ornaments to be attached to the coffin or casket, including coffin plates, engraved with the name and dates of the deceased, handles, armorial shields, and symbols such as crosses or flowers. They were made of various metals, including solid silver, silver plate, zinc, or silvered pressed tin. Long strips of ornamental metal were called "coffin lace." Coffin plates were sometimes removed just before burial and given to the family as a memento. They might be framed and displayed on the wall of the best parlor.

Consecrated Ground: Ground blessed in a ceremony of consecration and set aside for Christian burials. Suicides and criminals were not buried in consecrated ground.

Corpse-candle: An omen of death which looked like a candle or flame floating in the air. They could be seen entering a house where a death would soon occur or moving along the path where a coffin would be carried to the graveyard.

Epitaph: An inscription on a tombstone or grave to memorialize the deceased.

Falls: The narrow streamers on the back of a widow's white cap. Also known as WEEPERS.

Featherman: A funeral attendant who carried a tray of plumes above his head in grand funeral processions, in imitation of the plumed helmet carried at a knightly funeral. They were considered to be extravagant and old-fashioned by the late nineteenth century.

Good Death: An ideal death, with family arranged around the deathbed, wills made, bequests distributed, farewells said, and no unfinished business.

Hairwork: Jewelry or pictures made with human hair. These were made as memorials for the dead or as sentimental love tokens. There were books of instruction on how to weave hair into bracelets, brooches, earrings, and rings. Braided or woven hair was often incorporated into mourning jewelry. Chopped hair was mixed with paint or glue to create memorial pictures. "Live" hair, cut from a living person, was considered better to work with than "dead hair."

Half-mourning: This was the period between deep mourning (usually all black with crape) and easing back into an ordinary wardrobe. Etiquette thought it was too shocking to society for the bereaved to go from deepest mourning to none. Colors such as grey, white, purple, violet, and mauve were worn. See MOURNING.

Immortelles: 1) dried flowers often used in funeral arrangements; 2) floral arrangements of white porcelain, displayed under glass domes on graves; 3) beaded French funeral wreaths.

Miasmas: Foul and oppressive smells that were believed to cause or spread disease.

Morgue / Dead House: A public building where the dead were taken to be stored or identified. For much of the nineteenth century, the public was admitted to view unidentified corpses laid out on slabs, behind glass, with their clothing hung up beside them, to assist in identification. Germany also had "waiting morgues," to make sure that the dead were actually dead before they were buried. Corpses were laid out with a wire attached to a finger, which, if the person stirred, would ring a bell to alert the attendants. It does not appear that any of these alarms ever detected a living person.

Mortsafe: A metal cage, coffin, or box placed around a wooden coffin to protect the contents from body snatchers. The metal was believed to make it more difficult to break into the coffin. Parishes had their own mortsafes, which were reused after the body had decayed enough so that it was no longer of use to the anatomy teachers. It is a myth that the iron cages were used to keep vampires from rising from the grave.

Mourning: Mourning had the following stages: full mourning, second mourning, and half-mourning. The length of time in each was calculated by how close one was to the deceased or by what the etiquette book consulted decreed. See APPENDIX for examples of mourning times.

Deep or Full Mourning: Dull black fabrics, lots of crape, long veil for widow for street wear, widow's cap for inside. No jewelry, no lace, no feathers, no velvet.

Second or Lightened Mourning: Often after 6 months or 1 year from the date of death, the widow might wear shinier black fabrics, less crape, perhaps some jewelry/lace/jet trimmings. This was also called "slighting" one's mourning. Half-mourning came after this period. See HALF-MOURNING.

Pall: A decorative piece of cloth used to cover a coffin or casket. Palls might be owned by the parish church, by an aristocratic family, by a guild or fraternal organization, or provided by an undertaker.

Pallbearer: One who assists in carrying a coffin or casket to the hearse or to the grave. Friends of the deceased were traditionally asked to assist with this duty and were often given mourning badges, mourning bands, rings, gloves, or scarves to commemorate the dead. Child pallbearers carried the coffins of their friends to the grave.

Parish: See CHURCH OF ENGLAND.

Pauper's Grave/ Potter's Field: Criminals, the unknown dead, and the poor who could not afford a funeral were buried at public expense in a pauper's grave. Paupers' graves were located in a cemetery or part of a cemetery called a Potter's Field. There is debate over the origins of this term. The most plausible suggests that "potter" was an early word for vagrant or stranger. A pauper's burial was a mark of shame. The poor paid into BURIAL CLUBS and sometimes went into debt to avoid being buried by the parish.

Premature Burial: The idea, much feared for most of the nineteenth century, that one would be buried alive. Medical science did not always know how to tell if life was completely extinct and it was probable that some "dead" people revived in their coffins. See SAFETY COFFIN.

Ruche: A ruffle or frill of white fabric fastened at the edge of a widow's bonnet. It was generally thought to relieve the black of the bonnet, which was not flattering to the face.

"Sad Hour" Clock: A representation of a clock face showing the time of death for the deceased. These could be made of embossed cardboard with moveable hands that would be inserted into a floral arrangement, often in the shape of a clock, to be displayed at the wake, viewing, funeral, or grave. Metal coffin plates were also made with moveable hands and the legend, "The Sad Hour." Sad Hour clock faces were sometimes carved or cast on tombstones.

Safety Coffin: A coffin designed to alert cemetery authorities that a person had been buried alive. Some sent up a flag or rang a bell and opened an air tube to the coffin. It is difficult to know how many of these were actually installed—the signal devices were designed to be removed after it was obvious that the person was actually dead.

Séance: A gathering of people, usually Spiritualists, to try to make contact with the dead. A "talking board," such as a Ouija board could be used or messages could be tapped out by the movements of a small table. A "medium," a person who claims to communicate with spirits, might also go into a trance and bring messages from the Afterlife or produce spirit gifts like flowers, known as apports.

Typhoid Fever: A deadly disease caused by bacteria, spread by contaminated water or food. It was believed that Prince Albert, Queen Victoria's husband, died of typhoid fever and her son, Prince Edward, nearly died of it a few years later.

Vault: A burial place usually beneath a church or cathedral. These sometimes had shelves or compartments to hold coffins or coffins might be stacked one on top of each other. A vault is also a rectangular box, usually of cement or concrete, placed over a coffin to prevent the grave from sinking as the coffin decays.

Wake: A watch or vigil by the body as long as it remained unburied. It was thought that the dead person should not be left alone, as a matter of respect. Wakes were often social occasions where drinking, singing, games, and courting went on through the night. The wake had nothing to do with making sure the person didn't turn into a vampire, nor was it to make sure that the person wasn't buried alive.

Weed(s): 1) The widow or widower's entire set of mourning clothing; 2) a long scarf of crape worn around a mourning man's hat, now only seen on Victorian-style undertakers; 3) a mourning band placed around a man's hat; 4) any fabric worn for mourning.

Widow's Cap: A cap worn to signify that a woman was a widow. They were usually made of lightweight, sheer white fabrics like tarlatan, tulle, or muslin, although some widows wore black caps. The caps we recognize from images of Queen Victoria had a "widow's peak" in the center. These were called Marie Stuart or Mary Stuart-style. Widow's caps had long streamers or lappets that hung down the back or framed the face.

Winding Sheet: A sheet used to wrap around a corpse, often tied at head and foot. Also, a sheet used to line a coffin, whose ends were laid over the corpse.

Bibliography

General

Connell, Brian and Adrian Miles. *The City Bunhill Burial Ground, Golden Lane, London: Excavations at South Islington Schools, 2006*. London, UK: Museum of London Archaeology, 2010.

Curl, James Stevens. *The Victorian Celebration of Death*. Stroud, UK: Sutton Pub., 2000.

Dowd, Quincy L. *Funeral Management and Costs: A World-Survey of Burial and Cremation*. Chicago, Illinois: The University of Chicago Press, 1921.

Fletcher, Kami and Ashley Towle. *Grave History: Death, Race, and Gender in Southern Cemeteries*. Athens, Georgia: University of Georgia Press, 2023.

Frank, Robin Jaffee. *Love and Loss: American Portrait and Mourning Miniatures*. New Haven, Connecticut: Yale University Art Gallery, 2000.

Friend, Craig Thompson and Lorri Glover. *Death and the American South*. New York, New York: Cambridge University Press, 2017.

Gittings, Clare and Peter C. Jupp. *Death in England: An Illustrated History*. New Brunswick, New Jersey: Rutgers University Press, 2000.

Jalland, Pat. *Death in the Victorian Family*. Oxford, UK: Oxford University Press, 1996.

Jamieson, Ross W. "Material Culture and Social Death: African-American Burial Practices." *Historical Archaeology*, 29 (4) 1995: pp. 39–58. *JSTOR*, http://www.jstor.org/stable/25616423. (Accessed 23 July, 2023.)

Laderman, Gary. *The Sacred Remains: American Attitudes Towards Death, 1799-1883*. New Haven, Connecticut: Yale University Press, 1996.

Meyer, Richard E. *Cemeteries and Gravemarkers: Voices of American Culture*. Logan, Utah: Utah State University Press, 1992.

Miles, Adrian, Brian Connell, and Museum of London. *New Bunhill Fields Burial Ground Southwark: Excavations at Globe Academy, 2008*. London, UK: Museum of London Archaeology, 2012.

Morley, John. *Death, Heaven, and the Victorians.* Pittsburgh, Pennsylvania: University of Pittsburgh Press, 1971.

Parsons, Brian. *The London Way of Death*. Stroud, UK: Sutton, 2001.

Puckle, Bertram S. *Funeral Customs: Their Origin and Development*. London, UK: T. Werner Laurie Ltd., 1926.

Reeve, Jez and Max Adams. *Across the Styx*. Walmgate, York, UK: Council for British Archaeology, 1993.

Richardson, Ruth. *Death, Dissection and the Destitute.* Chicago, Illinois: University of Chicago Press, 2000.

Rose, Jerome Carl and Arkansas Archeological Survey. *Gone to a Better Land: A Biohistory of a Rural Black Cemetery in the Post-Reconstruction South*. Fayetteville, Arkansas: Arkansas Archeological Survey, 1985.

Springate, Megan E. *Coffin Hardware in Nineteenth-Century America*. Walnut Creek, California: Left Coast Press, 2015.

Strange, Julie-Marie. *Death, Grief and Poverty in Britain, 1870-1914*. Cambridge, UK: Cambridge University Press, 2005.

Vlach, John Michael. "Graveyard Decoration," *The Afro-American Tradition in Decorative Arts*. Cleveland, Ohio: Cleveland Museum of Art, 1978.

Woodyard, Chris. *The Victorian Book of the Dead*. Dayton, Ohio: Kestrel Publications, 2014.

Arsenic

Browne, G. Lathom. *Reports of Trials for Murder by Poisoning.* London, UK: Stevens and Sons, 1883.

https://www.gutenberg.org/files/50636/50636-h/50636-h.htm (Accessed 21 July, 2023.)

Emsley, John. "Whatever Happened to Arsenic?" *New Scientist.* December 26, 1985: pp. 10-14.
http://johnemsley.com/articles/new_scientist/ns_arsenic.html (Accessed 21 July, 2023.)

Hartman, Mary S. *Victorian Murderesses: A True History of Thirteen Respectable French and English Women Accused of Unspeakable Crimes*. Mineola, New York: Dover Publications, 2021.

Hempel, Sandra. *The Inheritor's Powder: A Tale of Arsenic, Murder, and the New Forensic Science*. New York, New York: W.W. Norton & Company, 2013.

Irving, Henry B. *Trial of Mrs. Maybrick.* Philadelphia, Pennsylvania: Cromarty Law Book, 1912.

MacGowan, Douglas. *The Strange Affair of Madeleine Smith: Victorian Scotland's Trial of the Century*. Edinburgh, UK: Polygon, 2021.

Parascandola, John. *King of Poisons: A History of Arsenic.* Washington, D.C: Potomac Books, 2012.

Sale of Arsenic Regulation Act, 1851.
https://www.legislation.gov.uk/ukpga/1851/13/contents/enacted (Accessed 21 July, 2023.)

Bier

Dottridge Brothers Ltd. Undertakers, Warehousemen & Manufacturers. *General Catalogue [of Coffins and Mortuary Fittings].* London, UK: Dottridge Brothers, Ltd., 1925.

Fitzgerald, Daniel. Improvement in Biers. United States. No. 38,575. Patent Issued 19 May, 1863.
https://patents.google.com/patent/US38575A/en?q=(bier+coffin)&oq=-bier+coffin&sort=old (Accessed 29 July, 2023.)

Parsons, Brian. *The Undertaker at Work: 1900-1950*. London, UK: Strange Attractor Press, 2014.

Scarlett, William. Bier. United States. No. 30,251. Patent Issued 2 October, 1860.
https://patents.google.com/patent/US30251A/en?q=(bier+coffin)&oq=-bier+coffin&sort=old (Accessed 21 July, 2023.)

Crape

Cole, George S. *A Complete Dictionary of Dry Goods and History of Silk, Cotton, Linen, Wool and Other Fibrous Substances Including a Full Explanation of the Modern Processes of Spinning, Dyeing and Weaving, with an Appendix Containing a Treatise on Window Trimming, German Words and Phrases, with Their English Pronunciation and Signification, Together with Various Useful Tables.* Chicago, Illinois: W.B. Conkey, 1892.

Coleman, D.C. *Courtaulds: An Economic and Social History.* Oxford, UK: Clarendon Press, 1969.

Taylor, Lou. *Mourning Dress: A Costume and Social History.* London, UK: Routledge, 2010.

Woodyard, Chris. "The Bold Crape Buyer: 1817." *The Victorian Book of the Dead.* 3 November, 2021.
https://thevictorianbookofthedead.wordpress.com/2021/11/03/the-bold-crape-buyer-1817 (Accessed 21 July, 2023.)

___. "Crape: A short story from *A Spot of Bother: Four Macabre Tales." Mrs Daffodil Digresses.*
https://mrsdaffodildigresses.wordpress.com/2013/09/01/crape-a-short-story-from-a-spot-of-bother-four-macabre-tales (Accessed 30 July, 2023.)

Death Token

Frisby, Helen. "'Them Owls Know': Portending Death in Later Nineteenth- and Early Twentieth-Century England." *Folklore.* 126 (2) 2015: pp. 196–214. *JSTOR.*
http://www.jstor.org/stable/24774310. (Accessed 22 July, 2023.)

___. *Traditions of Death and Burial.* Oxford, UK: Shire Publications, 2019.

Woodyard, Chris. "A Banshee in Indiana." *The Victorian Book of the Dead,* 18 January, 2023.
https://thevictorianbookofthedead.wordpress.com/2023/01/18/a-banshee-in-indiana-1877 (Accessed 21 July, 2023.)

___. "The Funeral Coach: 1855." *The Victorian Book of the Dead.* 13 October, 2021.
https://thevictorianbookofthedead.wordpress.com/2021/10/13/the-funeral-coach-1855 (Accessed 21 July, 2023.)

___. "The Funeral Men: 1856." *The Victorian Book of the Dead.* 21 October, 2020.
https://thevictorianbookofthedead.wordpress.com/2020/10/21/the-funeral-men-1856 (Accessed 21 July, 2023.)

___. "Phantom Funerals." *Haunted Ohio Books.* 21 March, 2013.
http://hauntedohiobooks.com/news/phantom-funerals (Accessed 21 July, 2023.)

___. "Tokens of Death: Owls, Cats, and Phantom Funerals." *Haunted Ohio Books.* 27 November, 2012.
http://hauntedohiobooks.com/news/tokens-of-death-owls-cats-and-phantom-funerals (Accessed 21 July, 2023.)

Embalming

Cincinnati College of Mortuary Science. "History."
https://www.ccms.edu/about-ccms/history/history/#:~:text=A%20leader%20in%20funeral%20service%20education%20since%201882!&text=To%20meet%20this%20need%2C%20our,father%20of%20American%20embalming%20schools.%E2%80%9D (Accessed 21 July, 2023.)

Dobson, Jessie. "Some Eighteenth Century Experiments in Embalming." *Journal of the History of Medicine and Allied Sciences* 8 (4) 1953: 431–41.
http://www.jstor.org/stable/24619780 (Accessed 29 July, 2023.)

Dodge, Asa Johnson. *The Practical Embalmer. A Common-Sense Treatise on The Art and Science of Embalming.* Boston, Massachusetts: The Author, 1900.
https://books.google.com/books?id=zcErAQAAMAAJ&printsec=frontcover&dq=intitle:embalming+inauthor:dodge&hl=en&newbks=1&newbks_redir=0&sa=X&ved=2ahUKEwit-tiaqaGAAxUyFFkFHfVNAs4Q6AF6BAgHEAI#v=onepage&q&f=false (Accessed 21 July, 2023.)

Michel, Gustav H., Dr. *The Scientific Embalmer; A Treatise on Judicial Embalming, Throwing Light on Very Important Questions Which Had So Far Remained Obscure.* Cleveland, Ohio: Dr. G.H. Michel & Co., 1913.
https://archive.org/details/thescientificemb00mich (Accessed 29 July, 2023.)

Nunnamaker, Albert John and Charles O. Dhonau. *Anatomy and Embalming: A Treatise on the Science and Art of Embalming, the Latest and Most Successful Methods of Treatment and the General Anatomy Relating to This Subject*. Cincinnati, Ohio: The Embalming Book Company, 1913.
https://www.gutenberg.org/files/49054/49054-h/49054-h.htm (Accessed 29 July, 2023.)

Picone, Louis L. *The President Is Dead!: The Extraordinary Stories of the Presidential Deaths, Final Days, Burials, and Beyond.* New York, New York: Skyhorse Publishing, 2016.

Renouard, Auguste. *The Undertakers' Manual: A Treatise of Useful and Reliable Information; Embracing Complete and Detailed Instructions for the Preservation of Bodies; Also the Most Approved Embalming Methods; with Hints on the Profession of Undertaking*. Rochester, New York: A.H. Nirdlinger, 1878.
https://www.gutenberg.org/cache/epub/70908/pg70908-images.html (Accessed 29 July, 2023.)

Woodyard, Chris. "Pickled to Death." *The Victorian Book of the Dead*. 16 May, 2018.
https://thevictorianbookofthedead.wordpress.com/2018/05/16/pickled-to-death (Accessed 13 July, 2023.)

___. "Lady Embalmers: 1893-1921." *The Victorian Book of the Dead*. 14 November, 2018.
https://thevictorianbookofthedead.wordpress.com/2018/11/14/lady-embalmers-1893-1921 (Accessed 13 July, 2023.)

Fisk Burial Case

Coachbuilt. "Crane & Breed." [n.d.] *coachbuilt.com*
http://www.coachbuilt.com/bui/c/crane_breed/crane_breed.htm (Accessed 22 July, 2023.)

Crane, Breed & Company. *Fisk's and Crane's Patent Metallic Burial Cases and Caskets: Air-Tight and Indestructible, for Protecting and Preserving the Dead, for Vaults, Transportation, Ordinary Interment, or Future Removal.* Cincinnati, Ohio: 1858.

"Edith Howard Cook." Wikipedia, last modified July 2021,
https://en.wikipedia.org/wiki/Edith_Howard_Cook (Accessed 22 July, 2023.)

Fisk, A.D., Improvement in Coffins. United States. No. 5920. Patent Issued 14 November, 1848.
https://patents.google.com/patent/US5920A/en?q=fisk&q=coffin&o-q=fisk+coffin (Accessed 21 July, 2023.)

Mytum, Harold and Laurie E. Burgess. *Death Across Oceans: Archaeology of Coffins and Vaults in Britain, America, and Australia.* Washington, D.C.: Smithsonian Institution Scholarly Press and Smithsonian Institution, 2018.

Serna, Joseph. "Mystery Solved: Remains of Girl in Forgotten Casket was Daughter of Prominent San Francisco Family." Los Angeles, California: *Los Angeles Times.* 10 May, 2017.
https://www.latimes.com/local/lanow/la-me-ln-miranda-metal-casket-girl-identified-20170509-htmlstory.html (Accessed 22 July, 2023.)

Warnasch, Scott. "Death, Burial and Iron Coffins." *Secrets of the Dead.* 21 September, 2018.
https://www.pbs.org/wnet/secrets/blog/death-burial-and-iron-coffins/ (Accessed 21 July, 2023.)

___. "Martha Peterson." *Iron Coffin Mummy.* [n.d.]
https://ironcoffinmummy.com/mummies/martha-peterson/ (Accessed 22 July, 2023.)

Wescott, Daniel J., Kelly Brinsko, Marina Faerman, Stephanie D. Golda, Jeff Nichols, Mark Spigelman, Bob Stewart, Margaret Streeter, Robert H. Tykot, and Ljuba Zamstein. "A Fisk Patent Metallic Burial Case from Western Missouri: An Interdisciplinary and Comprehensive Effort to Reconstruct the History of an Early Settler of Lexington, Missouri." *Archaeological and Anthropological Sciences* 2 (4) 2010: 283–305. doi:10.1007/S12520-010-0045-9.
https://www.academia.edu/199581/A_Fisk_Patent_Metallic_Burial_Case_from_western_Missouri_a_interdisciplinary_and_comprehensive_effort_to_reconstruct_the_history_of_an_early_settler_of_Lexington_Missouri?email_work_card=title (Accessed 29 July, 2023.)

Gates Ajar

Kemp, Ben. "A Necessary Undertaking." *Grantcottage.org.* 29 July, 2019.
https://www.grantcottage.org/blog/2019/7/29/a-necessary-undertaking (Accessed 24 July, 2023.)

Phelps, Elizabeth Stuart Fields. *The Gates Ajar*. Boston, Massachusetts: Fields Osgood, 1869.
https://books.google.com/books?id=Iv8EAAAAYAAJ&printsec=frontcover&dq=%22gates+ajar%22&hl=en&sa=X&ved=0ahUKEwjJieCv6N-jZAhXxqFkKHS9hDtgQ6AEIKTAA#v=onepage&q=%22gates%20ajar%22&f=false (Accessed 21 July, 2023.)

Hearse

Crane, Breed & Company. *Illustrated Catalogue of Hearses, Undertaker's Wagons, Emblems, Etc.* Cincinnati, Ohio: Crane, Breed & Company, 1878.

D'Amato, Michael P. and Carriage Museum of America. *Horse-Drawn Funeral Vehicles: 19th Century Funerals*. Bird-in-Hand, Pennsylvania: Carriage Museum of America, 2004.

Litten, Julian. *The English Way of Death: The Common Funeral Since 1450*. London, UK: Robert Hale, 2002.

McCall, Walter M. P. *American Funeral Vehicles, 1883-2003: An Illustrated History*. Hudson, Wisconsin: Iconografix, 2003.

Scott N. M. *The British Hearse and the British Funeral: A Pictorial History*. Brighton, UK: Book Guild, 2011.

Woodyard, Chris. "Hearse Horses." *The Victorian Book of the Dead*. 2 January, 2019.
https://thevictorianbookofthedead.wordpress.com/2019/01/02/hearse-horses (Accessed 13 July, 2023.)

___. "Hell-Wain Spotting." *The Victorian Book of the Dead*. 6 November, 2019.
https://thevictorianbookofthedead.wordpress.com/2019/11/06/hell-wain-spotting (Accessed 16 August, 2023.)

Ice Box

Johnson, H.C. Corpse Cooler and Preserver. United States. No. 311,764. Patent Issued 3 February, 1885.
https://patents.google.com/patent/US311764?oq=%22corpse+cooler%22 (Accessed 13 July, 2023.)

Mott, M.E. Corpse Preserver. United States No. 78,314. Patent Issued 26 May, 1868. https://patents.google.com/patent/US78314A/en?q=burial+garment&before=priority:19181231&after=priority:18400101&sort=old&page=2 (Accessed 13 July, 2023.)

Nash, George W. Improvement in Corpse-Preservers. United States. No. 115,229. Patent Issued 23 May, 1871. https://patents.google.com/patent/US115229A/en?q=burial+garment&before=priority:19181231&after=priority:18400101&sort=old&page=2 (Accessed 13 July, 2023.)

Reed, A.G. Corpse Cooler. United States No. 105,368. Patent Issued 12 July, 1870. https://patents.google.com/patent/US105368A/en?q=glass+coffin&oq=glass+coffin&sort=old (Accessed 13 July, 2023.)

Woodyard, Chris. "Corpses on Ice: The Dangers of the Undertaker's Ice-Box." *The Victorian Book of the Dead.* 10 July, 2019. https://thevictorianbookofthedead.wordpress.com/2019/07/10/corpses-on-ice-the-dangers-of-the-undertakers-ice-box (Accessed 13 July, 2023.)

___. "A Stiff Drink." *Haunted Ohio Books.* 28 July, 2016. http://hauntedohiobooks.com/grim-and-grewsome/11744 (Accessed 25 July, 2023.)

Jet

Kendall, Hugh P. *The Story of Whitby Jet.* [n.p.]: Horne and Son, 1936.

McMillan, Mabel. *Whitby Jet through the Years.* Whitby, UK: Mabel McMillan, 1992.

Muller, Helen. *Jet Jewellery and Ornaments.* Princes Risborough, Buckingham, UK: Shire, 2008.

Muller, Helen and Katey Scrace. *Whitby Jet.* Oxford, UK: Shire, 2009.

Nehama, Sarah, Anne E. Bentley, and Massachusetts Historical Society. *In Death Lamented: The Tradition of Anglo-American Mourning Jewelry.* Boston, Massachusetts: Massachusetts Historical Society, 2012.

Peters, Hayden. "Discover Whitby Jet." *Art of Mourning.* [n.d.]
https://artofmourning.com/discover-whitby-jet/?fbclid=IwAR3hDw-Z3zDdnTYrKBU9CBCJ8ufoAUhYTfjSywpIGQxq30_LhVHM4_mGot3c (Accessed 22 July, 2023.)

Whitby Museum, North Yorkshire, England. "Jet and Jet Jewellery."
https://whitbymuseum.org.uk/collection/jet-and-jet-jewellery (Accessed 29, July, 2023.)

Whitworth Alan. *Whitby Jet: A Brief History*. Whitby, UK: Culva House Publications, 2005.

Keen

Brady, Andrea. "To Weep Irish: Keening and the Law." In *Law and Mourning.* Martha Merrill Umphrey, ed. Amherst, Massachusetts: University of Massachusetts Press, 2017. Pp. 59–93.
https://www.academia.edu/41658396/_To_Weep_Irish_The_Politics_of_Early_Modern_Keening_ (Accessed 29 July, 2023.)

Croker Thomas Crofton. *The Keen of the South of Ireland: As Illustrative of Irish Political and Domestic History, Manners, Music, and Superstitions*. London, UK: Printed for the Percy Society by T. Richards. 1844.
https://archive.org/details/keenofsouthofire00crok (Accessed 29 July, 2023.)

Dúchas.ie. The Schools' Collection. "Old Customs." The Schools' Collection. Volume 0733, Page 084.
https://www.duchas.ie/en/cbes/5009070/4983653/5117076. (Accessed 5 June, 2023.)

Gallagher, Kitty. "27 Keen for a Dead Child [song] – Kitty Gallaghery / Cití Ní Ghallchóir, Gweedore, O. Donegal." 1951 *YouTube.*
https://www.youtube.com/watch?v=Mf7KleM2Ojs (Accessed 29 July, 2023.)

Lysaght, Patricia. *The Banshee: The Irish Death-Messenger*. Boulder, Colorado: Roberts Rinehart, 1997.

McLaughlin, Mary. "Keening the Dead: Ancient History or a Ritual for Today?" *Religions* 10 (4) 2019. p. 235.
https://www.mdpi.com/2077-1444/10/4/235 (Accessed 29 July, 2023.)

LibraryIreland. "O'G.: The Irish Funeral Cry (the Ullaloo, Keeners and Keening)." *Dublin Penny Journal.* 1 (31) 26 January, 1833.
https://www.libraryireland.com/articles/IrishFuneralCryDPJ1-31/ (Accessed 29 July, 2023.)

Lychgate

Messent, Claude John Wilson, *Lych-gates and Their Churches in Eastern England: South Lincolnshire, Norfolk, Suffolk, North Essex and East Cambridgeshire, Their Environments*. Blofield, Norwich, UK: C.J.W. Messent, 1970.

Vallance, A. *Old Crosses and Lychgates*. London, UK: Batsford, 1933.

Mutes

May, Trevor. *The Victorian Undertaker.* Princes Risborough, Buckingham, UK: Shire Publications Ltd, 1996.

Wood, Claire. *Dickens and the Business of Death*. Cambridge, UK: Cambridge University Press, 2015.

Necropolis

Broun, Sir Richard. *Extramural Sepulture: Synopsis of the London Necropolis and National Mausoleum at Woking.* London, UK: Trelawney Saunders, 1851.

Clarke, John M. *The Brookwood Necropolis Railway.* Usk, UK: Oakwood Press, 2006.

___. *London's Necropolis: A Guide to Brookwood Cemetery*. Stroud, UK: Sutton, 2006.

Dawes, M.C. *The End of the Line: The Story of the Railway Service to the Great Northern London Cemetery*. Barnet, UK: Barnet & District Local History Society, 2003.

Holmes, Mrs. Basil [Isabella]. *The London Burial Grounds,* London, UK: T. Fisher Unwin, 1896.
https://www.gutenberg.org/ebooks/56832 (Accessed 22 July, 2023.)

Slade, Paul. "Last Train Home: The Necropolis Railway." *Planetslade.com.*
http://www.planetslade.com/necropolis-railway.html (Accessed 25 July, 2023.)

Wheatley, Nicolas. *Final Journey: The Untold Story of Funeral Trains*. History Press, 2020.

Obelisk

Curl, James Stevens. *The Egyptian Revival: An Introductory Study of a Recurring Theme in the History of Taste*. London, UK: G. Allen & Unwin, 1982.

Giguere, Joy M. *Characteristically American: Memorial Architecture, National Identity, and the Egyptian Revival*. Knoxville, Tennessee: University of Tennessee Press, 2014.

"Gravestones and Symbolism." *Wilson Center Digilab*. Athens, Georgia: University of Georgia: [n.d.]
https://digilab.libs.uga.edu/cemetery/exhibits/show/history/symbols (Accessed 29 July, 2023.)

Post Mortem

Burns, Stanley B. *Sleeping Beauty: Memorial Photography in America*. Altadena, California: Twelvetrees Press, 1990.

Burns, Stanley B. and Elizabeth A. Burns. *Sleeping Beauty II: Grief, Bereavement and the Family in Memorial Photography: American & European Traditions*. New York, New York: Burns Archive Press, 2002.

Burns, Stanley B. and Burns Archive. *Sleeping Beauty III: Memorial Photography. The Children: Selections from the Burns Collection & Archive*. New York, New York: Burns Archive Press, 2011.

Cruz Lichet, Virginia de la. *El Retrato Y La Muerte: La Tradición De La Fotografía "Post Mortem" En España*. Madrid, Spain: Temporae, 2013.

Hollander, Stacy C., Gary Laderman, Anne-Imelda Radice and American Folk Art Museum. *Securing the Shadow: Posthumous Portraiture in America*. New York, New York: American Folk Art Museum, 2016.

Lesy, Michael, Charles Van Schaick and Warren Susman. *Wisconsin Death Trip*. Albuquerque, New Mexico: University of New Mexico Press, 2000.

Meinwald, Dan. "*Memento Mori*: Death and Photography in Nineteenth-Century America." *California Museum of Photography (CMP) Bulletin*. 9 (4) University of California, Riverside, Terminals project, [n.d.].
http://vv.arts.ucla.edu/terminals/meinwald/meinwald1.html (Accessed 23 July, 2023.)

Mord, Jack. *Beyond the Dark Veil: Post-Mortem & Mourning Photography from the Thanatos Archive*. San Francisco, California: Last Gasp, 2014.

Ruby, Jay. *Secure the Shadow: Death and Photography in America*. Cambridge, Massachusetts: MIT Press, 1999.

Woodyard, Chris. "Dead Man Standing." *The Victorian Book of the Dead*. 15 May, 2019.
https://thevictorianbookofthedead.wordpress.com/2019/05/15/dead-man-standing (Accessed 13 July, 2023.)

___. "Photographing the Dying: 1891." *The Victorian Book of the Dead*. 17 May, 2023.
https://thevictorianbookofthedead.wordpress.com/2023/05/17/photographing-the-dying-1891 (Accessed 13 July, 2023.)

___. "Pictures of the New York Morgue: 1876." *The Victorian Book of the Dead*. 1 March, 2023.
https://thevictorianbookofthedead.wordpress.com/2023/03/01/pictures-of-the-new-york-morgue-1876 (Accessed 13 July, 2023.)

___. "Taking Pictures of the Dead: An Interview with a Photographer: 1882." *The Victorian Book of the Dead*. 29 June, 2022.
https://thevictorianbookofthedead.wordpress.com/2022/06/29/taking-pictures-of-the-dead-an-interview-with-a-photographer-1882 (Accessed 13 July, 2023.)

Queen Victoria

Coulter, John and John A. Cooper. *Queen Victoria: Her Grand Life and Glorious Reign*. Chicago, Illinois: Neil, 1901.

Erskine, Mrs Steuart, editor. *Twenty Years at Court, 1842-1862 from the Correspondence of the Hon. Eleanor Stanley, Maid of Honour to Her late Majesty Queen Victoria 1842-1862*. London, UK: Nisbet & Co. Ltd., 1916.

Fulford, Roger. *Dearest Child; Letters between Queen Victoria and the Princess Royal, 1858-1861*. New York, New York: Holt, Rinehart and Winston, 1964.

Goldthorpe, Caroline and Costume Institute (New York, N.Y.). *From Queen to Empress: Victorian Dress 1837-1877: An Exhibition at the Costume Institute December 15 1988-April 16 1989*. New York, New York: Metropolitan Museum of Art, 1988.

Rennell, Tony. *Last Days of Glory: The Death of Queen Victoria*. New York, New York: St. Martin's Press, 2001.

Tooley, Sarah A. Southall. *The Personal Life of Queen Victoria*. New York, New York: Dodd Mead, 1897.

Resurrection Men

Adams, Norman. *Dead and Buried?: The Horrible History of Bodysnatching*. Aberdeen, UK: Bell Publishing Co., 1972.

Bailey, James Blake. *The Diary of a Resurrectionist, 1811-1812: To Which Are Added an Account of the Resurrection Men in London and a Short History of the Passing of the Anatomy Act*. London, UK: Swan Sonnenschein & Co., 1896.
https://www.gutenberg.org/files/32614/32614-h/32614-h.htm (Accessed 30 July, 2023.)

Clover, Philip K. Coffin-Torpedo. United States. No. 208,672. Patent Issued 8 October, 1878.
https://patents.google.com/patent/US208672?oq=coffin+torpedo+clover (Accessed 22 July, 2023.)

Cole, Hubert. *Things for the Surgeon: A History of the Resurrection Men*. London, UK: Heinemann, 1964.

Dalton, Curt. *Body Snatching in Ohio: A Century of Digging Up Corpses in the Buckeye State*. Dayton, Ohio: The Author, 2020.

___. *The Terrible Resurrection*. Dayton, Ohio: The Author, 2002.

Drimmer, Frederick. *Body Snatchers, Stiffs, and Other Ghoulish Delights*. New York, New York: Fawcett, 1981.

Edwards, Linden F. *Body Snatching in Ohio During the Nineteenth Century,* 1950. https://resources.ohiohistory.org/ohj/search/display.php?page=75&ip-p=20&searchterm=hildreth&vol=59&pages=329-351 (Accessed 22 July, 2023.)

___. *Cincinnati's "Old Cunny": A Notorious Purveyor of Human Flesh.* Fort Wayne, Indiana: Public Library of Fort Wayne and Allen County, 1955.

Juettner, Otto. *Daniel Drake and His Followers.* Cincinnati, Ohio: Harvey Publishing Company, 1909.

Lanum, R.B. Grave-Torpedo. United States. No. 228,651. Patent Issued 8 June, 1880. https://patents.google.com/patent/US228651A/en?q=grave+robbing&o-q=grave+robbing&sort=old&page=1 (Accessed 22 July, 2023.)

Lennox, Suzie. *Bodysnatchers: Digging Up the Untold Stories of Britain's Resurrection Men.* Barnsley, South Yorkshire, UK: Pen & Sword History, 2016.

Richardson, Ruth. *Death, Dissection and the Destitute.* Chicago, Illinois: University of Chicago Press, 2001.

Schultz, Suzanne M. *Body Snatching: The Robbing of Graves for the Education of Physicians in Early Nineteenth Century America.* Jefferson, North Carolina: McFarland & Co., 2005.

Shroud

Act for 'Burying In Woollen Onley'. Heritage & Culture, Warwickshire, UK, November, 2014.
https://api.warwickshire.gov.uk/documents/WCCC-863-935#:~:text=The%20act%20required%20that%20all,the%20exclusion%20of%20foreign%20textiles (Accessed 13 July, 2023.)

Blackford, William Henry. Burial Garment. United States. No. 1,101,724. Filed 29 August, 1913. Patent Issued 30 June, 1914.
https://patents.google.com/patent/US1101724A/en?q=burial+garment&before=priority:19181231&after=priority:18400101 (Accessed 13 July, 2023.)

Cameron, Karen. "Dead Fashionable." *Coffin Works.* 8 July, 2020.
http://www.archive.coffinworks.org/volunteering/dead-fashionable/ (Accessed 13 July, 2023.)

Davidson, Hilary. "Grave Emotions: Textiles and Clothing from Nineteenth-Century London Cemeteries." *TEXTILE*, 14:2, 2016. Pp. 226-243.
https://www.researchgate.net/publication/304617918_Grave_Emotions_Textiles_and_Clothing_from_Nineteenth-Century_London_Cemeteries (Accessed 29 July, 2023.)

Hayes, Saran. "The Evolution of the English Shroud: From Single Sheet to Drawstrings and Sleeves." *Coffin Works.* 18 August, 2019.
http://www.archive.coffinworks.org/uncategorised/the-evolution-of-the-english-shroud-from-single-sheet-to-draw-strings-and-sleeves/ (Accessed 13 July, 2023.)

Holcomb, C.C. Burial Garment. United States. No. 1,028,464. Filed 18 May, 1906. Patent Issued 4 June, 1912.
https://patents.google.com/patent/US1028464A/en?q=burial+garment&oq=burial+garment&page=1 (Accessed 13 July, 2023.)

Litten, Julian. *The English Way of Death: The Common Funeral Since 1450*. London, UK: Robert Hale, 2002.

Rice, B. Front for Burial Robe. United States. No. 212,265. Patent Issued 11 February, 1879.
https://patents.google.com/patent/US212265A/en?q=(burial+garment)&before=priority:19181231&after=priority:18400101&sort=old&page=6 (Accessed 13 July, 2023.)

Woodyard, Chris. "The Death Drawer: 1900." *The Victorian Book of the Dead.* 13 March, 2018.
https://thevictorianbookofthedead.wordpress.com/2018/03/13/the-death-drawer-1900 (Accessed 22 July, 2023.)

___ . "Mother Made Baby's Shroud: 1904." *The Victorian Book of the Dead.* 8 September, 2021.
https://thevictorianbookofthedead.wordpress.com/2021/09/08/mother-made-babys-shroud-1904 (Accessed 22 July, 2023.)

___. "Sewing Shrouds: 19th-century Burial Clothing." *The Victorian Book of the Dead.* 26 April, 2018.
https://thevictorianbookofthedead.wordpress.com/2018/04/26/sewing-shrouds-19th-century-burial-clothing (Accessed 13 July, 2023.)

Tear Bottle

Hearn, Candice. "Throwaway Scent Bottles." *Regency World at candicehern.com.* https://candicehern.com/regencyworld/throwaway-scent-bottles/ (Accessed 24 July, 2023.)

McBride, Nuri. "Victorian Tear Catchers Are Trash." *The Death Scent Project.* 5 August, 2021.
https://deathscent.com/2021/09/28/victorian-tear-catchers-are-trash/ (Accessed 13 July, 2023.)

Vatomsky, Sonya. "Debunking the Myth of 19th-Century 'Tear Catchers.' *Atlas Obscura.* 2 May, 2017.
https://www.atlasobscura.com/articles/tearcatchers-victorian-myth-bottle (Accessed 13 July, 2023.)

Woodyard, Chris. "Transparent Fiction—The Myth of the Victorian Tear Bottle." *The Victorian Book of the Dead.* 3 October, 2018.
https://thevictorianbookofthedead.wordpress.com/2018/10/03/transparent-fiction-the-myth-of-the-victorian-tear-bottle (Accessed 13 July, 2023.)

Undertaker

May, Trevor. *The Victorian Undertaker.* Princes Risborough, Buckingham, UK: Shire Publications Ltd, 1996.

Parsons, Brian. *The Undertaker at Work: 1900-1950.* London, UK: Strange Attractor Press, 2014.

Wood, Claire. *Dickens and the Business of Death.* Cambridge, UK: Cambridge University Press, 2015.

Woodyard, Chris. "A Lady Undertaker: 1912." *The Victorian Book of the Dead.* 31 August 2022.
https://thevictorianbookofthedead.wordpress.com/2022/08/31/a-lady-undertaker-1912 (Accessed 13 July, 2023.)

___. "Mortuary Professions for Ladies: 1889-1910." *The Victorian Book of the Dead.* 3 September, 2018.
https://thevictorianbookofthedead.wordpress.com/2018/09/03/mourning-professions-for-ladies-1889-1910 (Accessed 13 July, 2023.)

Veil

Cunnington, Phillis and Catherine Lucas. *Costume for Births, Marriages & Deaths.* New York, New York: Harper & Row: 1972.

Taylor, Lou. *Mourning Dress: A Costume and Social History*. London, UK: G. Allen and Unwin, 1983.

Weepers

Curl, James Stevens. *The Victorian Celebration of Death.* Stroud, UK: Sutton Pub., 2000.

Morley, John. *Death, Heaven, and the Victorians.* Pittsburgh, Pennsylvania: University of Pittsburgh Press, 1971.

Taylor, Lou. *Mourning Dress: A Costume and Social History*. London, UK: G. Allen and Unwin, 1983.

X-Sexton

Woodyard, Chris. "The Angel of Gettysburg: Elizabeth Thorn: 1863." *The Victorian Book of the Dead.* 30 June, 2021.
https://thevictorianbookofthedead.wordpress.com/2021/06/30/the-angel-of-gettysburg-elizabeth-thorn-1863 (Accessed 13 July, 2023.)

___. "A Ghastly Traffic in Grave-Clothes: 1862, 1878." *The Victorian Book of the Dead.* 18 September, 2019.
https://thevictorianbookofthedead.wordpress.com/2019/09/18/a-ghastly-traffic-in-grave-clothes-1862-1878 (Accessed 22 July, 2023.)

___. "A Grave Man: The Sexton of Spring Grove: 1866." *The Victorian Book of the Dead.* 11 November, 2020.
https://thevictorianbookofthedead.wordpress.com/2020/11/11/a-grave-man-the-sexton-of-spring-grove-1866 (Accessed 30 July, 2023.)

___. "Gravediggers on Strike: 1916." *The Victorian Book of the Dead.* 29 July, 2021.
https://thevictorianbookofthedead.wordpress.com/2021/07/29/gravediggers-on-strike-1916 (Accessed 13 July, 2023.)

Y-Churchyard

Amadei, Gian Luca. *Victorian Cemeteries and the Suburbs of London: Spatial Consequences to the Reordering of London's Burials in the Early 19th Century*. New York, New York: Routledge, Taylor & Francis Group, 2022.

Bailey Brian J. *Churchyards of England and Wales*. Leicester, UK: Magna Books, 1994.

Barker, Felix. *Highgate Cemetery: Victorian Valhalla*. Salem, New Hampshire: Merrimack, 1985.

Brooks, Chris. *Mortal Remains: The History and Present State of the Victorian and Edwardian Cemetery*. Exeter, UK: Wheaton, 1989.

Chadwick, Edwin, Great Britain Home Office and Great Britain Poor Law Commissioners. *Report on the Sanitary Conditions of the Labouring Population of Great Britain. A Supplementary Report on the Results of a Special Inquiry into the Practice of Interment in Towns. Made at the Request of Her Majesty's Principal Secretary of State for the Home Department*. London, UK: Printed by W. Clowes and Sons for H.M. Stationery Off., 1843.
https://books.google.com/books?id=0QDPAAAAMAAJ&printsec=-frontcover&dq=intitle:report+intitle:on+intitle:the+intitle:sanitary+in-title:conditions+inauthor:chadwick&hl=en&newbks=1&newbks_redir=0&sa=X&ved=2ahUKEwi5na_i66OAAxUWD1kFHXC-5Ck4Q6AF6BAgHEAI#v=onepage&q&f=false (Accessed 22 July, 2023.)

Curl, James Stevens. *The Victorian Celebration of Death*. Stroud, UK: Sutton Pub., 2000.

Holmes, Mrs. Basil [Isabella]. *The London Burial Grounds*. London, UK: T. Fisher Unwin, 1896.
https://www.gutenberg.org/ebooks/56832 (Accessed 22 July, 2023.)

Meller, Hugh. *London Cemeteries: An Illustrated Guide and Gazetteer*. Stroud, UK: History Press, 2022.

Walker, George Alfred. *Gatherings from Grave Yards; Particularly Those of London: With a Concise History of the Modes of Interment among Different Nations from the Earliest Periods, and a Detail of Dangerous and Fatal Results Produced by the Unwise and Revolting Custom of Inhuming the Dead in the Midst of the Living*. London, UK: Longman and Company, 1839.

Woodyard, Chris. "Appalling Scenes at Spa-Fields Burial Ground: 1845." *The Victorian Book of the Dead.* 12 April, 2023.
https://thevictorianbookofthedead.wordpress.com/2023/04/12/appalling-scenes-at-spa-fields-burial-ground-1845 (Accessed 13 July, 2023.)

Zinc

Fisher, Marc. "Why Those Confederate Soldier Statues Look a Lot Like Their Union Counterparts." *Washington Post.* 18 August, 2017.
https://www.washingtonpost.com/politics/why-those-confederate-soldier-statues-look-a-lot-like-their-union-counterparts/2017/08/18/cefcc1bc-8394-11e7-ab27-1a21a8e006ab_story.html (Accessed 11 July, 2023.)

Grissom, Carol A. *Zinc Sculpture in America 1850-1950*. Newark, Delaware: University of Delaware Press, 2009.

Monumental Bronze Co. *White Bronze Monuments, Statuary, Portrait Medallions, Busts, Statues, and Ornamental Art Work: For Cemeteries, Public and Private Grounds and Buildings Manufactured by the Monumental Bronze Co. of Bridgeport, Conn.*
https://library.si.edu/digital-library/book/whitebronzemonu00monu (Accessed 11 July, 2023.)

Paxson, Comfort and Company. *White Bronze Monuments and Statuary: Medallions, Portrait Busts &c. for Cemeteries, Public and Private Grounds.* Philadelphia, Pennsylvania: Paxson Comfort, 1878.
https://babel.hathitrust.org/cgi/pt?id=nnc2.ark:/13960/s25kbt1hzv6&view=1up&seq=1 (Accessed July 12, 2023.)

Rotundo, Barbara. "Monumental Bronze: A Representative American Company." In *Cemeteries and Gravemarkers: Voices of American Culture.* Richard E. Meyer, ed. Logan, Utah: Utah State University Press, 1992.

Web Resources

These sites and museums offer more information on the topics in brackets.

Braintree District Museum has displays, artifacts, and an archive relating to Courtauld & Co., which began in Braintree. [See CRAPE.]
https://www.braintreemuseum.co.uk/courtauld-co/ (Accessed 13 August, 2023.)

The Brookwood Cemetery Society. The Society offers regular guided tours, including one which follows the route of the old rail line in Brookwood Cemetery. [See NECROPOLIS.]

www.tbcs.org.uk (Accessed 2 August, 2023.)

Clarke, John M. Historian of Brookwood Cemetery and its railway funeral service. [See NECROPOLIS.]

https://www.john-clarke.co.uk/index.html (Accessed 2 August, 2023.)

The Coffin Works, home of Newman Brothers Coffin Furniture Manufactory, makers of coffin furniture and shrouds. [See SHROUD.]

https://www.coffinworks.org (Accessed 2 August, 2023.)

Dúchas.ie. The Schools' Collection. National Folklore Collection to collect, preserve and disseminate the oral tradition of Ireland. [See KEEN.]

https://www.dúchas.ie/en/info/cbe (Accessed 2 August, 2023.)

National Funeral Museum UK. A history of death at the heart of East London. [See UNDERTAKER.]

https://nationalfuneralmuseum.wordpress.com (Accessed 2 August, 2023.)

National Museum of Funeral History, America's largest collection of authentic, historical funeral service items. [See HEARSE.]

https://www.nmfh.org (Accessed 2 August, 2023.)

Peters, Hayden, a Jewellery Historian, Scholar and Designer. A resource for mourning and sentimental jewels. [See JET.]

https://artofmourning.com (Accessed 2 August, 2023.)

The Thanatos Archive. Early Post Mortem & Memorial Photography [See POST MORTEM.]

www.Thanatos.net (Accessed 2 August, 2023.)

The Victorian Book of the Dead Blog. The popular and material culture of Victorian death and mourning, selected by Chris Woodyard, author of *The Victorian Book of the Dead*. [See ALL ABC ENTRIES.]

https://thevictorianbookofthedead.wordpress.com (Accessed 2 August, 2023.)

The Whitby Museum, with exhibits on the Whitby jet industry. [See JET.]

https://whitbymuseum.org.uk (Accessed 29 July, 2023.)

About the Author

Chris Woodyard is an historian of death and the supernatural. Author of *The Victorian Book of the Dead*, *The Ghost Wore Black: Ghastly Tales from the Past*, plus 9 books on Ohio ghostlore, including the *Haunted Ohio* series. Chris co-hosts "Boggart and Banshee: A Supernatural Podcast" with Simon Young.

Blog: https://thevictorianbookofthedead.wordpress.com

Facebook: The Victorian Book of the Dead, Haunted Ohio by Chris Woodyard

Instagram: chriswoodyard1295

Podcast: Boggart and Banshee: A Supernatural Podcast

Twitter: @hauntedohiobook

YouTube: Ghost and Grave

Woman in Black by Jessica Wiesel.

About the Illustrator

Landis Blair is the illustrator and author of *The Night Tent*, *Vers le Sud*, and *The Envious Siblings: and Other Morbid Nursery Rhymes*, as well as the illustrator of the New York Times bestseller *From Here to Eternity*, by Caitlin Doughty and the graphic novel *The Hunting Accident*, by David Carlson which won the 2021 Fauve d'Or and the 2020 Quai des Bulles prize. His illustrations have appeared in numerous print and online periodicals including *The New Yorker*, the *New York Times*, *Chicago magazine*, and Atlas Obscura. He lives in Chicago.

Milton Keynes UK
Ingram Content Group UK Ltd.
UKHW020627031124
2543UKWH00042B/246